YOU CAN TEACH YOURSELF
DRUMS

By James Morton

Contents

Introduction

If you are new to drumming, and to music in general, this book was written for you. If you have played another instrument before, you will probably find the lessons in this book easier to apply. Basic drumming concepts are introduced progressively, so that if you stick with it, you will have a good foundation upon which to further build your musicianship.

There are essentially four learning tracks presented in this book:

1. *Technique:* This incorporates the grip, sticking, and the methods used to achieve musical sounds. Technique can be viewed as a means to an end, and a serious musician will approach the study of technique with determination. You can save yourself lots of future headaches by paying particular attention to the pages devoted to technique. It is vastly preferable to develop good habits from the beginning, rather than spending many months afterwards trying to correct bad ones.

2. *Reading:* Music notation is the quickest way to convey a musical idea. It is the written language of musicians. Basic reading principles are introduced in this book in a logical sequence. I know that, if you are new to reading music, this can seem a little intimidating, like a foreign language. Reading rhythms is a little like reading fractions. Once you understand how things are broken down, it's really not that difficult.

3. *Writing:* Not many teachers include writing notation as part of their curriculum, but I think it is a very important part of one's musical development. By actually putting down on paper the rhythms you are currently struggling with, you develop an increasingly intimate awareness of the way notes and rests are arranged to create rhythms. Therefore, I have included review "worksheets" which include writing assignments. I hope you do them, for I have seen my own students become much better readers as a result.

4. *Application:* Putting what you know into practice is what counts in any learning situation, and in music this is where you will have the most enjoyment. After some basic principles are introduced, there will be an opportunity for you to apply them in musical contexts. There are six charts in this book for you to learn, each one representative of a standard rock style. And if you really enjoy playing with the musicians on the cassette, wait 'til you play in a band of your own! I always encourage my students to take the initiative and play with other musicians, because that's when they really take off. They're having so much fun, they forget they are learning at the same time! Don't think that you have to wait until you are "good enough." There are plenty of guitarists and keyboardists out there who are just like you. In fact, they're probably wondering where *you* are.

I've enjoyed playing the drums for over 25 years now, ever since, as a boy of 13, I took my paper-route money and ordered a drum set through the Sears catalog. It was a red-sparkle cheapie, but I thought it was the coolest thing I could ever own. It was a greater thrill than even getting your own car. Or dating a cheerleader. And I still feel that way today! I hope you can take the excitement you feel, also (otherwise you wouldn't be reading this), and apply yourself to what follows. Happy drumming!

1964

Graphic Guides

At the beginning of each lesson, there are graphic displays that are intended to clarify your understanding of the lesson. In the upper right corner of the first page of each lesson is a boxed list of objectives for that lesson, like this:

> **Quarter Note and Rest**
> **Half Note and Rest**
> **Whole Note and Rest**

Above that, there is a small drawing of a standard five-piece drum set, shown from above, like this:

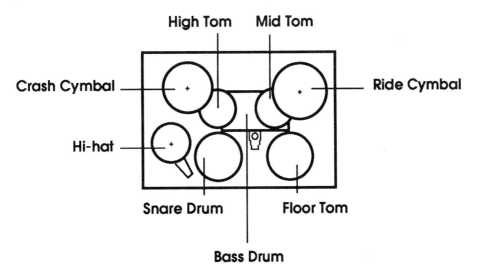

The parts of the drum set which are to be used during that lesson will be shaded, like so:

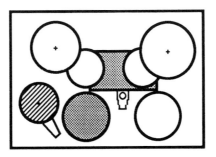

And, finally, those sections of the book which are recorded on the accompanying cassette tape are indicated by this symbol:

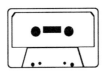

Being a Drummer: A Job Description

There are lots of jobs in the world, and all of them come with job descriptions. A job description lists the duties that a particular job entails. Well, you would be surprised at the number of students who have not thought about what a drummer actually does. Most of us have seen a drummer that particularly inspired us, and that is what made us want to become drummers ourselves. But I do think it is helpful if we clearly list the skills necessary for a drummer to perform adequately. Knowing what you are aiming for will help you focus on the following lessons.

The Role of the Drummer

The role of the drummer can be broken down into three basic functions:

1. To rhythmically contribute to the flow of the music and offer rhythmic support to the other instruments. (In other words — keep the beat!)

2. To embellish the music with appropriate fills, breaks, and punches.

3. To solo when necessary.

These are the primary functions of a drummer. Here are two more that are a little more aesthetic:

4. To conceptualize the musical piece as a whole, being aware of its form and parts.

5. To listen to the other musicians carefully and respond appropriately.

I should point out that the above duties describe the role of any drummer, not just a rock drummer. Anyway, I hope this description clears up any misconceptions you may have had about being a drummer.

How to Hold the Sticks

Most rock drummers use what is called the "matched grip" (the left-hand grip is the same as the right-hand grip; they are "matched"). Pick the drumstick up and hold it between the thumb and the first joint of the first finger. Now curve the other three fingers around the stick. Hold the stick securely, but not too tightly.

Lesson 1:
Some Basics

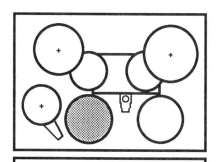

Basic Terms
Sticking Patterns

Basic Terms

Every kind of music, from a marching band to the latest rock band, is made up of three elements: *melody, harmony,* and *rhythm.* Since a drummer adds rhythmic support to music, his or her primary concern and contribution is **rhythm.** Rhythm is the first element of music.

If you have ever tapped your foot or clapped along with a song, you were feeling the **beat,** or underlying pulse of the music. In writing music, one way of indicating beats is by using a note like this:

This particular note is called the **quarter note,** and it is the note most often thought of as **one beat.** Therefore, when you see a quarter note, you will strike the drum **once.**

Other words to know:

> **Stroke:** A single, completed movement of the stick to the drum by the wrist.
>
> **Sticking:** The determination of which stick to use for each note. Sticking is indicated by the letters **R** and **L** (for guess what).
>
> **Staff:** Most music is written on a group of five parallel lines called a **staff.** Note that there are four spaces between the five lines. Traditionally, music for the snare drum is placed on the third space of the staff:
>
> Snare Drum →

As we progress through the following lessons, we will see how other parts of the drum set are notated.

Sticking Patterns

The following sticking patterns are basic to drumming, and they must be mastered and practiced regularly so they can be played with a smooth and fluid motion. For now, play these on the snare drum. Repeat each exercise several minutes without stopping.

1. SINGLE STROKES (Leading with the RH)

2. SINGLE STROKES (Leading with the LH)

3. DOUBLE STROKES (Leading with the RH)   *Double strokes* consist of two consecutive strokes on each hand. Make each stroke steady and precise.

4. DOUBLE STROKES (Leading with the LH)

5. PARADIDDLES   A *paradiddle* is a combination of single strokes and double strokes. Watch the sticking closely as you play.

We will continue developing single strokes, double strokes, and paradiddles throughout the following lessons. As stated earlier, these patterns are basic to drumming. You should practice them until the patterns are memorized and you can play them smoothly and reflexively. Later, we will practice them for speed.

Lesson 2:
Basic Reading

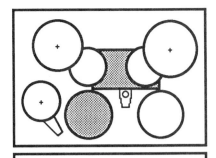

In Lesson 1, we learned that the note most often thought of as one beat is the quarter note:

In music, notes are organized in groups called **measures.** Measures are formed by vertical lines called **bar lines.** Look at Exercise 1 on the following page, and you will notice that each measure has exactly four beats. The amount of beats (or counts) to each measure is determined by the stacked numbers you see at the beginning of the exercise:

 = how many beats (counts) per measure
= indicates the quarter note receives one beat

This pair of numbers is called a **time signature.** The time signature always tells us how we are to count the music. Four/four time, which is the most commonly used time signature (most rock songs are in 4/4), simply means that there are four counts of quarter notes in each measure. Therefore, we will count each quarter note as we play it: "one, two, three, four, one, two," etc.

Note the double bar and dots at the end of Exercise 1:

This is called a **repeat sign.** A repeat sign directs us back to the beginning of the exercise, to play it once more.

As you play these exercises:

- Check for proper grip and position.
- Count the beats aloud as you play: 1,2,3,4,1,2,3,4, etc.
- Follow the indicated stickings. Alternating single strokes are to be used. Each exercise begins with the right stick, then alternates hand to hand.
- Make the notes even and precise. Keep the beat steady.
- Play steady quarter notes on the bass drum as you play the exercises. The bass drum is notated on the first space of the staff:

Bass Drum →

1. Count: 1 2 3 4 | 1 2 3 4 | 1 2 3 4 | 1 2 3 4
Play: R L R L | R L R L | R L R L | R L R L

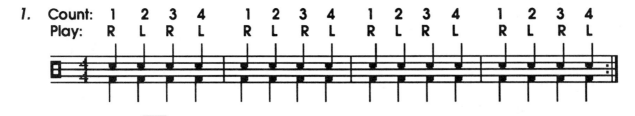

QUARTER REST You already know that a quarter note indicates a beat (or count) to be played. A **quarter rest** indicates a beat (or count) **not played**. A quarter rest has exactly the same time value as a quarter note, so this rest must be counted, even though it is not played.

2. Count: 1 2 3 4 | 1 2 3 4 | 1 2 3 4 | 1 2 3 4
Play: R L R – | L R L – | R L R – | L R L –

3. Count: 1 2 3 4 | 1 2 3 4 | 1 2 3 4 | 1 2 3 4
Play: – R L R | – L R L | – R L R | – L R L

4. Count: 1 2 3 4 | 1 2 3 4 | 1 2 3 4 | 1 2 3 4
Play: R – L R | L – R L | R – L R | L – R L

5. Count: 1 2 3 4 | 1 2 3 4 | 1 2 3 4 | 1 2 3 4
Play: R L – R | L R – L | R L – R | L R – L

6. Count: 1 2 3 4 | 1 2 3 4 | 1 2 3 4 | 1 2 3 4
Play: R – L – | R – L – | R – L – | R – L –

7. Count: 1 2 3 4 | 1 2 3 4 | 1 2 3 4 | 1 2 3 4
Play: – R – L | – R – L | – R – L | – R – L

HALF NOTE ♩ The **half note** is always twice as long as a quarter note. In 4/4 time, since a quarter note equals one beat, a half note is two beats long. Think of it as one note that lasts for two counts. Strike the half note once, but give it two beats.

8. Count: 1 2 3 4   1 2 3 4   1 2 3 4   1 2 3 4
Play: R   L   R L R L   R   L   R L R L

HALF REST ▬ Every type of note has a corresponding rest, which has the **same value** as that note. The **half rest,** like the half note, is also equal to two beats (in 4/4 time); but two beats you count, and do not play.

9. Count: 1 2 3 4   1 2 3 4   1 2 3 4   1 2 3 4
Play: R L – –   R L – –   R L R L   R L – –

WHOLE NOTE 𝅝 The **whole note** is always twice as long as a half note. In 4/4 time, since the half note is two beats long, the whole note is four beats long. Strike the drum once, but give it four counts.

10. Count: 1 2 3 4   1 2 3 4   1 2 3 4   1 2 3 4
Play: R – – –   L R L R   L – – –   R L R L

WHOLE REST ▬ Like the quarter and half notes, the whole note also has a corresponding rest. In 4/4 time, the **whole rest** occupies an entire measure. The whole rest, like the whole note, is equal to four beats; but four beats you count, but do not play.

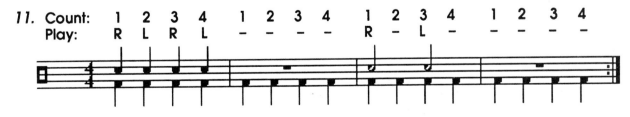

11. Count: 1 2 3 4   1 2 3 4   1 2 3 4   1 2 3 4
Play: R L R L   – – – –   R – L –   – – – –

COMBINATION EXERCISE   The following four-line exercise is a review of what you have learned so far. The sticking and counting are not indicated, so try to play and count on your own. Keep the beat steady as you play. Note what looks like a repeat sign without the dots at the end of the last measure. This is **not** a repeat, but indicates **the end** of the music.

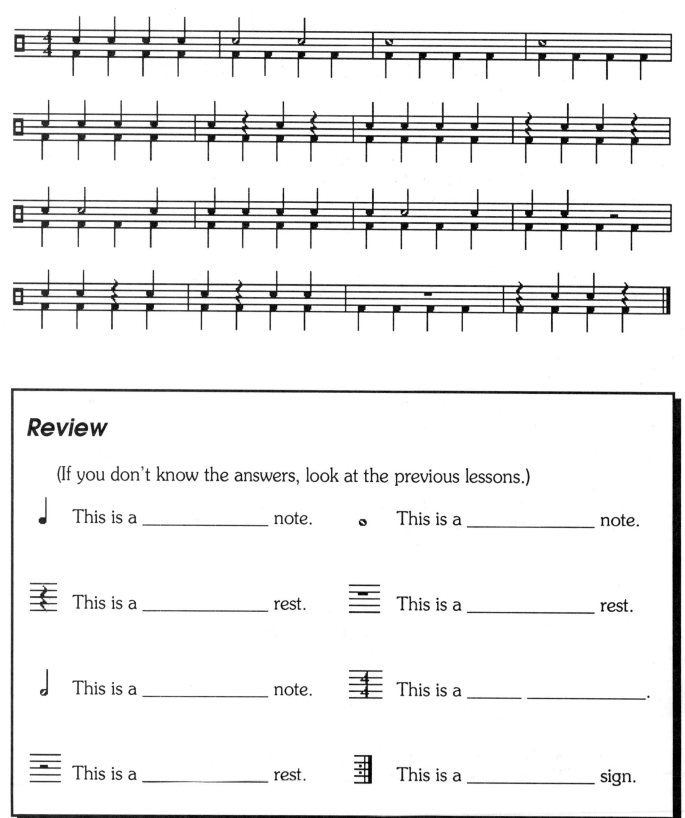

Review

(If you don't know the answers, look at the previous lessons.)

♩ This is a _____ note.   𝑜 This is a _____ note.

☰ This is a _____ rest.   ☰ This is a _____ rest.

♩ This is a _____ note.   ☰ This is a _____ _____.

☰ This is a _____ rest.   ☰ This is a _____ sign.

14

Lesson 3: Hand-and-Foot Coordination Exercises

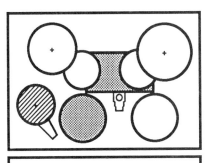

Hand/Foot Coordination

When you move from the snare to the set, the most obvious coordination factor to consider is how your hands and feet relate to each other. Most drum-set coordinational difficulties can be overcome with patient practice. The following exercises are meant to prepare you for subsequent lessons, which will deal in various beats, fills, and charts. Some hand-and-foot combinations fall more naturally than others (the RH falls against the RF more easily than against the LF, for example). The conscientious drummer will want to iron out any coordinational difficulties with persistent practice.

These exercises deal with playing the five sticking patterns you learned in Lesson 1 against different foot patterns. The notation for the hi-hat to be pedaled (not struck with the stick) with the LF is an "x" figure below the staff:

Hi-Hat (with LF)

Counting Tip: It is important for every musician to know at which measure he or she is at any time. You can get started on that now by playing each exercise eight times without stopping. To do this, count the quarter notes as you have done in the previous lesson, but this time substitute the "1" of each measure for the numbered repetition you are on: **1,** 2, 3, 4; **2,** 2, 3, 4; **3,** 2, 3, 4; **4,** 2, 3, 4; etc., sort of like counting running laps. Now you won't get lost.

EXERCISES 1–5   The five sticking patterns against bass-drum quarter notes.

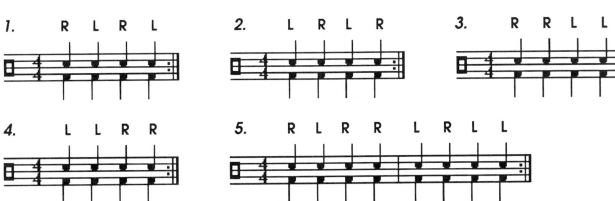

15

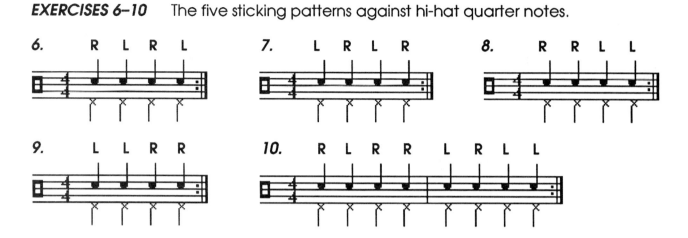

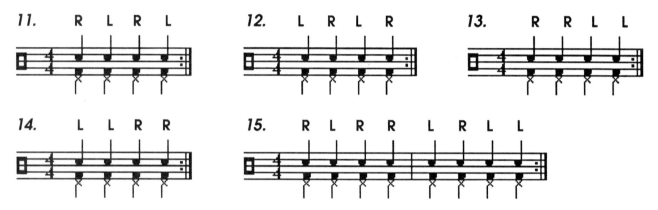

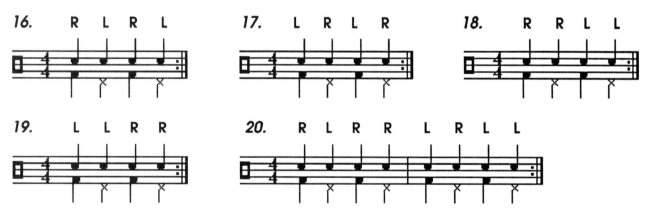

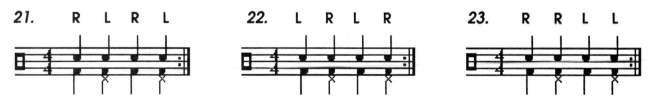

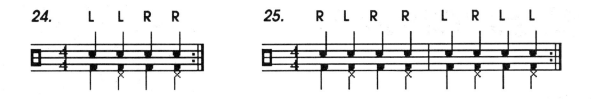

Advanced Challenge: Take any two of the five sticking patterns and stack them against each other, with the hands (on snare) playing the top sticking, and the feet (on bass drum and hi-hat) playing the bottom sticking. Good luck!

Some examples:

| RLRL | RLRL | RLRL | RRLL | RRLL | RLRR LRLL |
| LRLR | RRLL | LLRR | LLRR | LRLR | RRLL RRLL |

Lesson 4 : Basic Blues (Chart 1)

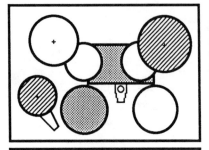

Quarter-Note Blues Beat
Extended Rest
Measure Repeat
Rehearsal Letters

Preparation

We are now coming to the fun part of learning music: actually playing! But first you have a few things to learn. In a few minutes, you should be playing the chart you see on page 20. If you look at the drum-set diagram above, you will notice that you will be playing the ride cymbal in addition to what you've used before (snare, bass drum, and hi-hat). The notation for the ride cymbal will be the "x" notation right above the staff. Here is the notation key to the extent we have gone so far:

Ride Cymbal (RH) ⟶   ⟵ Snare Drum (LH)

Bass Drum (RF) ⟶   ⟵ Hi-Hat (LF)

Here is the basic beat you will use throughout Chart 1:

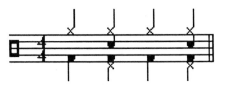

Note that the ride cymbal is a steady quarter-note pulse, as is the bass drum. Your right hand and your right foot play together. Note that the snare drum is on "2" and "4" (this is called the ***backbeat***), as is the hi-hat. Your left hand and your left foot play together.

Other new items:

Extended Rest: On the first line of the chart, right after the time signature, you'll see a thick bar with a number over it. In this case, you will enter after resting for four measures. You can count these rested measures just as you would if you were playing: **1,** 2, 3, 4; **2,** 2, 3, 4; **3,** 2, 3, 4; **4,** 2, 3, 4.

Measure Repeat: This is important, as often the charts I play have more of these than notes! A measure repeat looks like this:

When you see a measure repeat, you are directed to repeat the measure you just played. Often, as is the case here, you will see several measure repeats in succession. You simply repeat the original measure as many times as there are measure repeats. Often, the writer or arranger will place a parenthesized number above every second or fourth measure repeat to aid in your counting.

Rehearsal Letters: The boxed letters you see at certain points throughout a chart are called "rehearsal letters" (sometimes they are numbers, rather than letters). Rehearsal letters break up a piece of music into identifiable sections that make it easier to read and also easier to rehearse ("Let's take it from letter *D*").

Double Bar Line: A double bar line consisting of two thin lines indicates the end of a section of music:

Tie: The curved line extending from the ride-cymbal quarter note in the last measure indicates the cymbal to ring free, then fade.

Performance Notes: The music in Chart 1 is a standard form called the ***12-bar blues.*** The blues progression is an early form of jazz, and many early rock 'n roll hits are based on it. The blues still remain a viable vehicle for rock songs. After you've played the chart a few times with the cassette, you should have a sense of the 12-measure cycle. In the meantime, count carefully and play in a relaxed and flowing manner.

CHART 1   Basic Blues

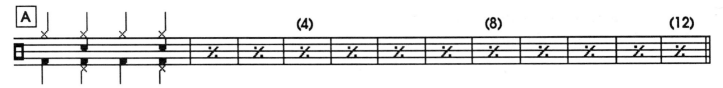

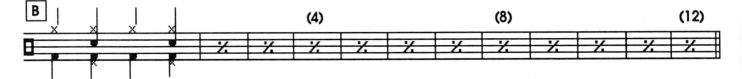

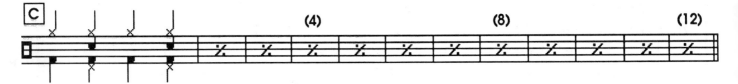

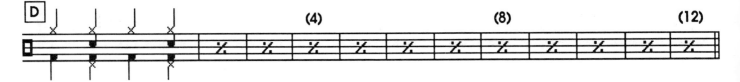

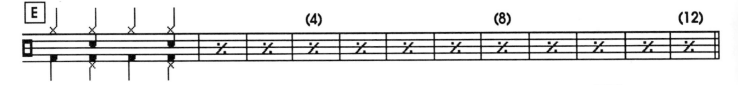

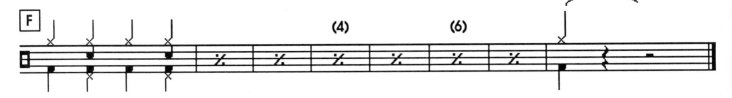

Lesson 5:
Eighth Notes

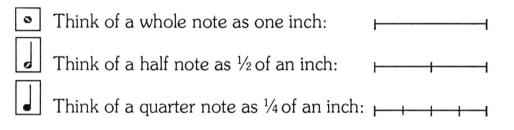

Eighth Notes

We now know three types of notes and their related rests: the whole note, the half note, and the quarter note. A good analogy for comparing the relationships of these three notes to each other is the measurement of an inch:

𝗼 Think of a whole note as one inch: ⊢————————————⊣

𝗱 Think of a half note as ½ of an inch: ⊢——————┼——————⊣

𝗱 Think of a quarter note as ¼ of an inch: ⊢——┼——┼——┼——⊣

In a sense, notes are used to measure time (or duration) the same way inches are used to measure length. Just as a whole note can be broken down into two half notes, a half note can be broken down into two quarter notes, and a quarter note can be broken down into two eighth notes.

Eighth notes are exactly twice as fast as quarter notes.

The eighth note looks like a quarter note with a flag attached. When they are written consecutively, eighth notes can also be joined together by a **beam:**

♪ ♪ = ♫

Note the relationship of quarter notes to eighth notes:

	1 2 3 4
Quarter Notes	♩ ♩ ♩ ♩
	1 + 2 + 3 + 4 +
Eighth Notes	♫♫♫♫

Note the indicated counting. We use the word "and" to account for the additional notes. The "ands" are to be played and counted **exactly** dead center between quarter notes. So, when eighth notes are to be played, we simply "double up" the beat. If quarter notes are one to the beat, eighth notes are two to the beat.

PREPARATORY EXERCISE   Look at this line. The first measure consists of quarter notes, while the second measure consists of eighth notes. The bass drum plays quarter notes throughout. You should practice this line repeatedly until you can easily feel the difference between quarter and eighth notes.

Count:	1	2	3	4	1 + 2 + 3 + 4 +
Play:	R	L	R	L	R L R L R L R L

Now go on to the following exercises.

1.

Count:	1 + 2 + 3 + 4 +	1 + 2 + 3 + 4 +	1 + 2 + 3 + 4 +	1 + 2 + 3 4
Play:	R L R L R L R L	R L R L R L R L	R L R L R L R L	R L R L R L

2.

Count:	1 + 2 + 3 4	1 + 2 + 3 4	1 + 2 + 3 4	1 + 2 + 3 4
Play:	R L R L R L	R L R L R L	R L R L R L	R L R L R L

3.

Count:	1 2 3 + 4 + 1	2 3 + 4 + 1	2 3 + 4 + 1	2 3 4
Play:	R L R L R L R	L R L R L R	L R L R L R	− L −

4.

Count:	1 + 2 3 4	1 + 2 3 4	1 + 2 3 4	1 + 2 3 4
Play:	R L R L R	L R L R L	R L R L R	L R L R L

5.

Count:	1 2 + 3 4	1 2 + 3 4	1 2 + 3 4	1 2 + 3 4
Play:	R L R L R	L R L R L	R L R L R	L R L R L

6.

Count:	1 2 3 + 4	1 2 3 + 4	1 2 3 + 4	1 2 3 + 4
Play:	R L R L R	L R L R L	R L R L R	L R L R L

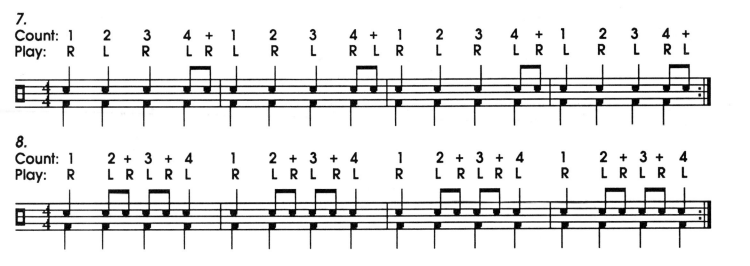

Lesson 6: Hand-and-Foot Coordination Exercises Using Eighth Notes

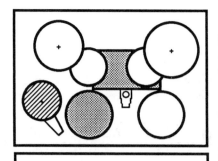

Hand/Foot Coordination
Exercises

Here are some further coordination exercises, this time using eighth notes against different foot patterns. Practice these until you can play them with a relaxed feel.

EXERCISES 1–5   The five sticking patterns as eighth notes against bass-drum quarter notes.

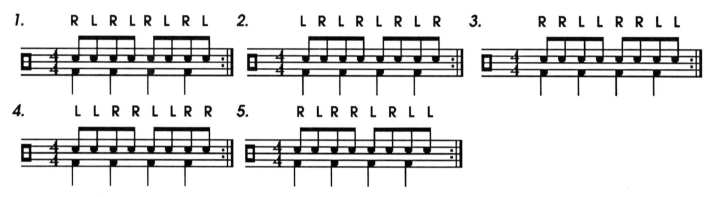

EXERCISES 6–10   The five sticking patterns as eighth notes against hi-hat quarter notes.

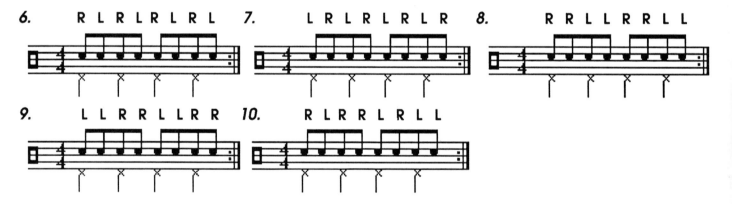

EXERCISES 11-15   The five sticking patterns played as eighth notes against BD and HH quarter notes played simultaneously.

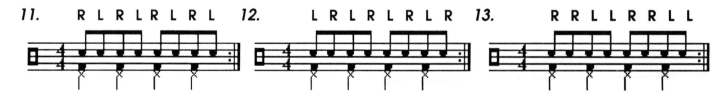

14. L L R R L L R R **15.** R L R R L R L L

EXERCISES 16–20 The five sticking patterns played as eighth notes against BD and HH alternating quarter notes.

16. R L R L R L R L **17.** L R L R L R L R **18.** R R L L R R L L

19. L L R R L L R R **20.** R L R R L R L L

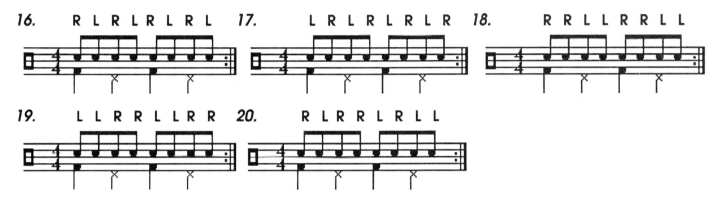

EXERCISES 21–25 The five sticking patterns played as eighth notes against BD quarter notes, HH on "2" and "4."

21. R L R L R L R L **22.** L R L R L R L R **23.** R R L L R R L L

24. L L R R L L R R **25.** R L R R L R L L

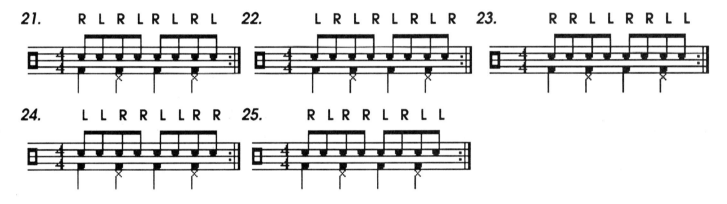

Lesson 7: Eighth Rests

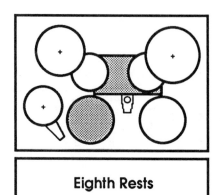

Eighth Rests

In this lesson, we will study the **eighth rest.** The eighth rest looks like this:

In previous lessons, you learned that every note has a corresponding rest with the same value. The eighth rest, therefore, has exactly the same value as the eighth note. It is important that you give the rests an equal amount of attention as you count these rhythms. Many drummers make the mistake of not paying enough attention to rests, and their reading suffers as a result. I advise you to count and "feel" the rests with the same intensity as you would count and "feel" the notes you play.

1.
Count: 1 + 2 3 4   1 + 2 3 4   1 + 2 3 4   1 2 3 4
Play: – R L R L   – R L R L   – R L R L   R L R L

2.
Count: 1 2 + 3 4   1 2 + 3 4   1 2 + 3 4   1 2 3 4
Play: R – L R L   R – L R L   R – L R L   R L R L

3.
Count: 1 2 3 + 4   1 2 3 + 4   1 2 3 + 4   1 2 3 4
Play: R L – R L   R L – R L   R L – R L   R L R L

4.
Count: 1 2 3 4 +   1 2 3 4 +   1 2 3 4 +   1 2 3 4
Play: R L R – L   R L R – L   R L R – L   R L R L

5.
Count: 1 + 2 + 3 + 4 +   1 + 2 + 3 + 4 +   1 + 2 + 3 + 4 +   1 2 3 4
Play: – R – L – R – L   – R – L – R – L   – R – L – R – L   R L R L

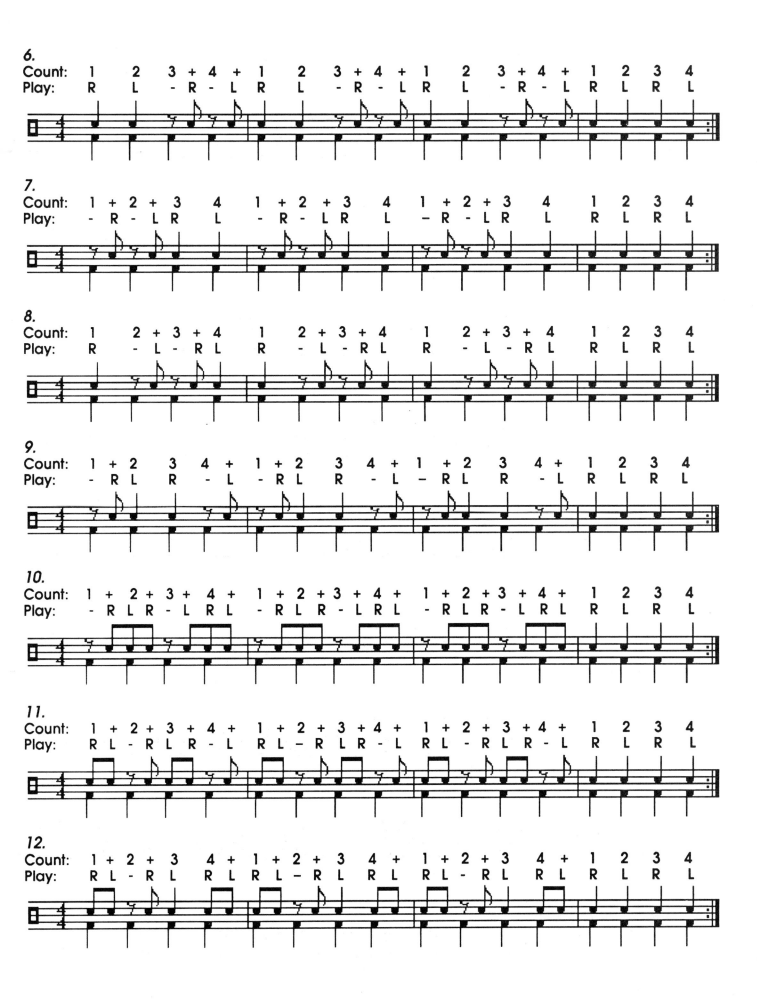

COMBINATION EXERCISE The following 32-measure study combines eighth notes and eighth rests. Make sure you can play this exercise accurately before you proceed. Refer to the cassette.

OTHER APPLICATIONS:
1. Play this exercise against the BD/HH patterns on pages 24 and 25.
2. Read this exercise vertically, in downward columns. (The measures are in alignment for this).

Review Worksheet

Look at this chart and answer the following questions:

Whole Note	
Half Notes	
Quarter Notes	
Eighth Notes	

1. One whole note is equal to two _____ notes. One whole note is equal to ____ (how many) quarter notes.

2. One half note is equal to ____ (how many) quarter notes.

3. The time signature 4/4 tells how many beats there are in each measure. In 4/4 time there are ____ (how many) beats to a measure.

4. Measures are created by vertical lines called bar lines. In the music below there are ____ (how many) measures.

5. Now copy the above line. Don't forget the time signature and bar lines:

6. You know three types of sticking patterns: single strokes, double strokes, and paradiddles. Identify these stickings:

RLRR LRLL   These are _____.

RLRL RLRL   These are _____.

RRLL RRLL   These are _____.

7. Draw a line from each rest to the proper corresponding note:

Lesson 8:
Eighth-Note Rock Beats

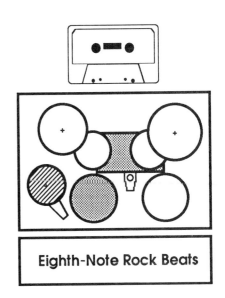

Eighth-Note Rock Beats

In this lesson you will be learning to play rock beats based on straight eighth notes. The most commonly used rock beats feature an **eighth-note ride pattern.** Play these eighth notes on the closed hi-hat, with your right hand crossing over. Play the snare drum part with your left hand, and of course the bass drum with your right foot. Align the bass drum and snare rhythm under the corresponding hi-hat note.

Here is the key to the notation used for this lesson:

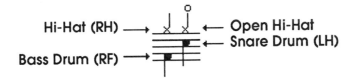

In addition to the notation given for each beat, there is also a set of boxes for each beat, as a visual aid. Each box relates to one eighth-note count of the rock beat. On top of each box is the count for that part of the beat. Inside each box are abbreviations for which parts of the drum set are used for that particular count of the beat. The abbreviations used inside the boxes are:

HH   Hi-hat, to be played with the cymbals closed, with the right hand.
HH-o Hi-hat, to be played with the cymbals opened, with the right hand.
SN   Snare drum, to be played with the left hand.
BD   Bass drum, to be played with the right foot.

If you have trouble either reading the notation or coordinating your limbs, following the boxes should help. Play each box one by one, and go slowly enough to do them correctly. You can pick up the tempo once you are sure of yourself. Once you have the beat mastered, transfer your attention back to the notation. Keep the beat steady, smooth, and relaxed. Repeat each beat eight times.

Notation:

Visual Key:

*1.
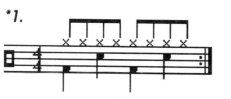

1	&	2	&	3	&	4	&
HH	HH	HH	HH	HH	HH	HH	HH
		SN				SN	
BD				BD			

*2.
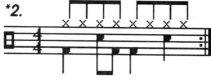

1	&	2	&	3	&	4	&
HH	HH	HH	HH	HH	HH	HH	HH
		SN				SN	
BD			BD	BD			

*3.
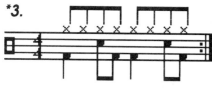

1	&	2	&	3	&	4	&
HH	HH	HH	HH	HH	HH	HH	HH
		SN				SN	
BD			BD	BD			BD

*4.
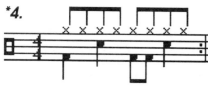

1	&	2	&	3	&	4	&
HH	HH	HH	HH	HH	HH	HH	HH
		SN				SN	
BD				BD	BD		

*5.

1	&	2	&	3	&	4	&
HH	HH	HH	HH	HH	HH	HH	HH
		SN				SN	
BD	BD			BD	BD		

*6.
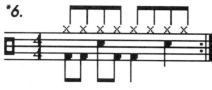

1	&	2	&	3	&	4	&
HH	HH	HH	HH	HH	HH	HH	HH
		SN				SN	
BD	BD		BD	BD			

*7.
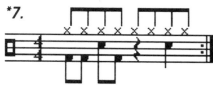

1	&	2	&	3	&	4	&
HH	HH	HH	HH	HH	HH	HH	HH
		SN				SN	
BD	BD		BD				

*8.
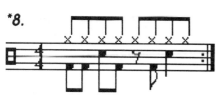

1	&	2	&	3	&	4	&
HH	HH	HH	HH	HH	HH	HH	HH
		SN				SN	
BD	BD		BD		BD		

Notation:

Visual Key:

*9.

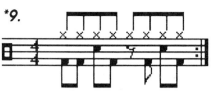

1	&	2	&	3	&	4	&
HH	HH	HH SN	HH	HH	HH	HH SN	HH
BD	BD		BD		BD		BD

*10.

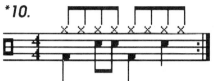

1	&	2	&	3	&	4	&
HH	HH	HH SN	HH SN	HH	HH	HH SN	HH
BD				BD			

*11.

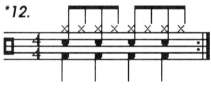

1	&	2	&	3	&	4	&
HH	HH	HH SN	HH	HH	HH	HH SN	HH SN
BD				BD			

*12.

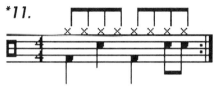

1	&	2	&	3	&	4	&
HH SN BD	HH	HH SN BD	HH	HH SN BD	HH	HH SN BD	HH

*13.

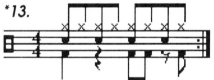

1	&	2	&	3	&	4	&
HH SN BD	HH	HH SN	HH	HH SN BD	HH BD	HH SN	HH BD

*14.

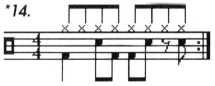

1	&	2	&	3	&	4	&
HH	HH	HH	HH SN	HH	HH SN	HH	HH SN
BD				BD	BD		

*15.

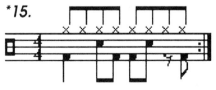

1	&	2	&	3	&	4	&
HH	HH	HH	HH SN	HH	HH SN	HH	HH
BD				BD	BD		BD

16.

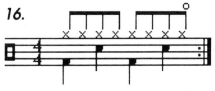

1	&	2	&	3	&	4	&
HH	HH	HH SN	HH	HH	HH	HH SN	HH-o
BD				BD			

Notation:

Visual Key:

17.
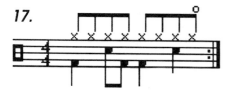

1	&	2	&	3	&	4	&
HH	HH	HH	HH	HH	HH	HH	HH-o
		SN				SN	
BD			BD	BD			

18.
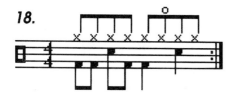

1	&	2	&	3	&	4	&
HH	HH	HH	HH	HH	HH-o	HH	HH
		SN				SN	
BD	BD		BD	BD			

*19.
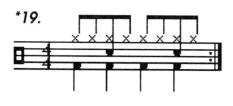

1	&	2	&	3	&	4	&
HH	HH	HH	HH	HH	HH	HH	HH
		SN				SN	
BD		BD		BD		BD	

20.
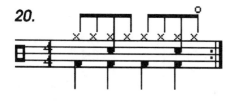

1	&	2	&	3	&	4	&
HH	HH	HH	HH	HH	HH	HH	HH-o
		SN				SN	
BD		BD		BD		BD	

21.
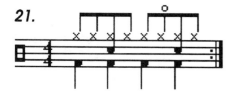

1	&	2	&	3	&	4	&
HH	HH	HH	HH	HH	HH-o	HH	HH
		SN				SN	
BD		BD		BD		BD	

22.
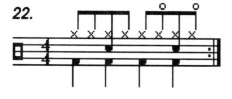

1	&	2	&	3	&	4	&
HH	HH	HH	HH	HH	HH-o	HH	HH-o
		SN				SN	
BD		BD		BD		BD	

23.
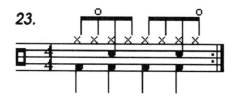

1	&	2	&	3	&	4	&
HH	HH-o	HH	HH	HH	HH	HH	HH-o
		SN				SN	
BD		BD		BD		BD	

24.
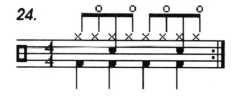

1	&	2	&	3	&	4	&
HH	HH-o	HH	HH-o	HH	HH-o	HH	HH-o
		SN				SN	
BD		BD		BD		BD	

*25.

1	&	2	&	3	&	4	&
HH	HH	HH SN	HH	HH	HH	HH SN	HH
	BD			BD	BD		BD

26.

1	&	2	&	3	&	4	&
HH	HH	HH SN	HH	HH	HH	HH SN	HH-o
	BD			BD	BD		BD

Two-Measure Patterns

*27.

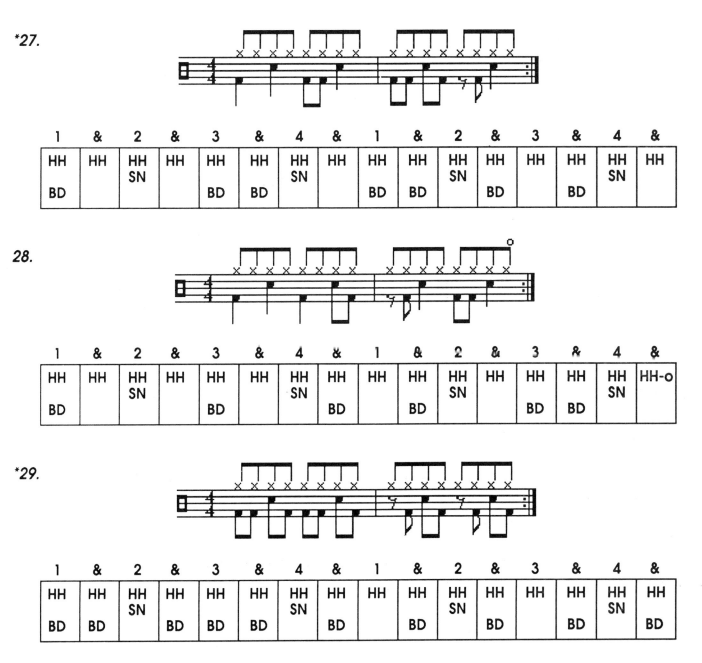

1	&	2	&	3	&	4	&	1	&	2	&	3	&	4	&
HH	HH	HH SN	HH	HH	HH	HH SN	HH	HH	HH	HH SN	HH	HH	HH	HH SN	HH
BD				BD	BD			BD	BD			BD		BD	

28.

1	&	2	&	3	&	4	&	1	&	2	&	3	&	4	&
HH	HH	HH SN	HH	HH	HH	HH SN	HH	HH	HH	HH SN	HH	HH	HH	HH SN	HH-o
BD				BD			BD		BD			BD	BD		

*29.

1	&	2	&	3	&	4	&	1	&	2	&	3	&	4	&
HH	HH	HH SN	HH	HH	HH	HH SN	HH	HH	HH	HH SN	HH	HH	HH	HH SN	HH
BD	BD		BD	BD	BD		BD	BD		BD	BD	BD		BD	BD

30.

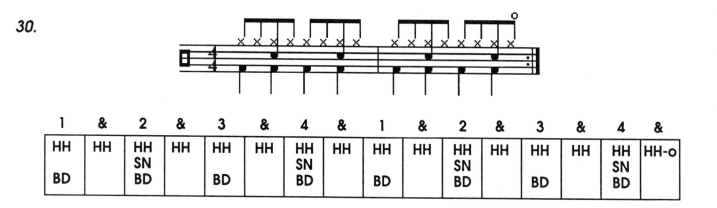

1	&	2	&	3	&	4	&	1	&	2	&	3	&	4	&
HH	HH	HH	HH	HH	HH	HH	HH	HH	HH	HH	HH	HH	HH	HH	HH-o
		SN				SN				SN				SN	
BD		BD		BD		BD		BD		BD		BD		BD	

Other Applications to Lesson 8 (Pages 31–35)

• Go over the previous eighth-note rock beats which have an asterisk (*) by the number. Place the eighth-note ride pattern on the ride cymbal. Now play each beat with the following hi-hat (left-foot) patterns. Observe that the notation for the pedaled (LF) hi-hat is an "x" note below the staff.

A. Hi-hat on "2" and "4."

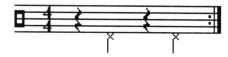

B. Hi-hat quarter notes.

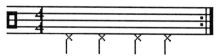

C. Hi-hat on offbeats ("ands").

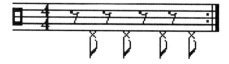

D. Hi-hat eighth notes.

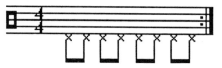

• Go over all 30 of the eighth-note rock beats. This time, reverse hands: LH on the hi-hat, RH on the snare. Many of the top drummers today are ambidextrous. They can lead with either hand. So, if you are serious about your drumming, you should try this variation, also.

• Practice changing from one beat to another. For instance, play beat #2 eight times, then go right into beat #7 without stopping. Play that eight times, then go into another beat, and so on.

• Create your own two-measure patterns (like those on page 35) by combining any two one-measure beats (#1– #26).

• Write your own eighth-note rock beats. Try writing the notation as well as the "box" method.

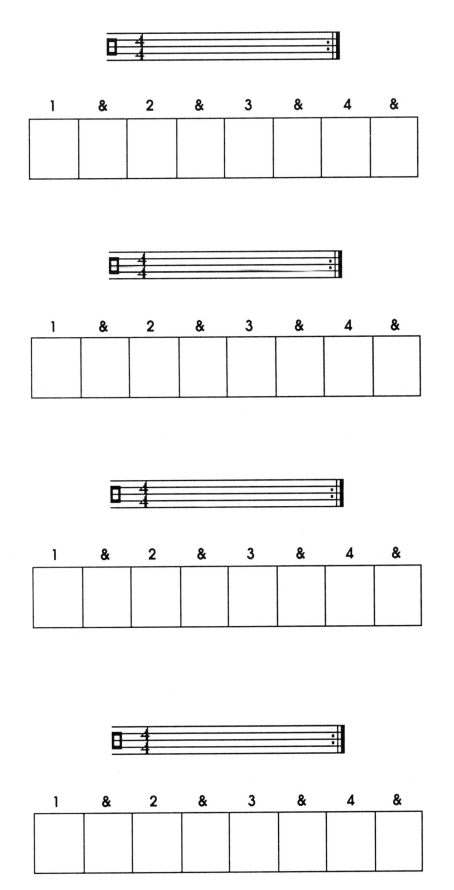

Lesson 9: Eighth-Note Rock (Chart 2)

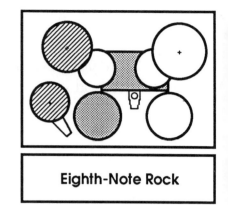

Preparation

You are now ready for your second chart. Chart 2 is a rock song with a basic feel that is straight eighth notes, the most common ride pattern found in rock. The basic beat used throughout the chart is one you learned in the last lesson:

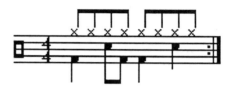

This pattern is probably the most common eighth-note rock beat. It has been used in *every* decade of rock's history on literally thousands of recordings. At *B*, the same pattern is played, except that the hi-hat is opened on the last eighth note of the measure:

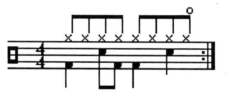

There is a new addition to our legend of notation, the cymbal crash:

Here is our legend of notation up to this point:

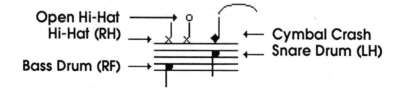

Performance Notes: As mentioned on the previous page, Chart 2 represents the most basic feel in rock music: the straight eighth-note ride pattern. Therefore, in order to make your drumming sound authentic, you should strive for a consistent sound and pulse on the hi-hat. A good musician listens for several things at once. As you hear yourself blending in with the other instruments, you should also be monitoring the consistency of *your* contribution. Play solid, steady, and relaxed!

CHART 2   *Eighth-Note Rock*

Lesson 10:
Sixteenth Notes

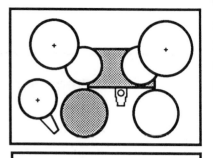

Sixteenth Notes

A quarter note can be broken down into two eighth notes:

An eighth note can be broken down into two sixteenth notes:

When we play eighth notes in 4/4 time, we are playing "two to the beat" — we are dividing the quarter note into two equal parts. When we play sixteenth notes in 4/4 time, we are playing "four to the beat" — we are dividing the quarter note into four equal parts. Therefore, one quarter note is equal to four sixteenth notes. **Sixteenth notes are twice as fast as eighth notes.**

Single sixteenth notes have two flags connected to the stem. In groups, they are joined by two beams. And now is as good a time as any for you to know the parts of a note:

Sixteenth notes are counted as follows (use a long "e" and a short "a" to count "One-ee-and-ah, Two-ee-and-ah," etc.):

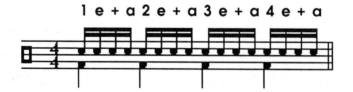

Practice playing and counting sixteenth notes against bass-drum quarter notes.

Now practice playing and counting the following exercise repeatedly, until the feel of sixteenth notes in relation to other notes is acquired. Keep your bass drum steady!

You are now ready to try the following exercises.

Lesson 11: Hand-and-Foot Coordination Exercises Using Sixteenth Notes

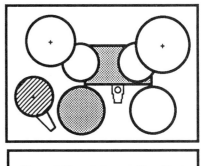

Hand/Foot Coordination Exercises

Here are some further coordination exercises, this time using sixteenth notes against different foot patterns. Practice these until you can play them with a relaxed feel.

EXERCISES 1–5 The five sticking patterns as sixteenth notes against bass-drum quarter notes.

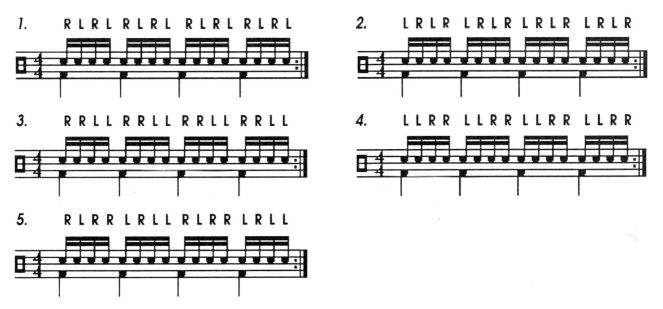

1. R L R L R L R L R L R L R L R L

2. L R L R L R L R L R L R L R L R

3. R R L L R R L L R R L L R R L L

4. L L R R L L R R L L R R L L R R

5. R L R R L R L L R L R R L R L L

EXERCISES 6–10 The five sticking patterns as sixteenth notes against hi-hat quarter notes.

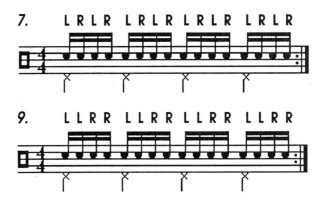

6. R L R L R L R L R L R L R L R L

7. L R L R L R L R L R L R L R L R

8. R R L L R R L L R R L L R R L L

9. L L R R L L R R L L R R L L R R

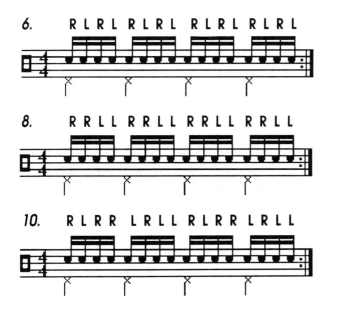

10. R L R R L R L L R L R R L R L L

EXERCISES 11–15   The five sticking patterns as sixteenth notes against BD and HH quarter notes played simultaneously.

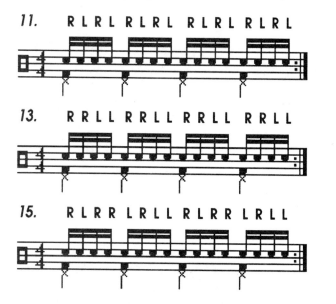

11.   R L R L R L R L R L R L R L R L

12.   L R L R L R L R L R L R L R L R

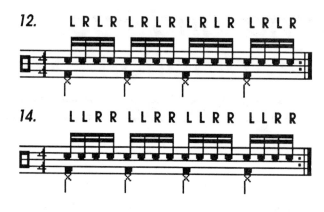

13.   R R L L R R L L R R L L R R L L

14.   L L R R L L R R L L R R L L R R

15.   R L R R L R L L R L R R L R L L

EXERCISES 16–20   The five sticking patterns played as sixteenth notes against BD and HH alternating quarter notes.

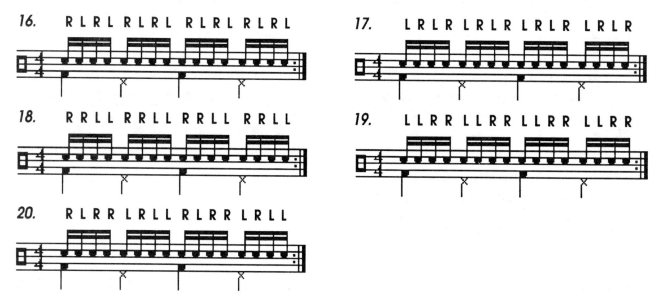

16.   R L R L R L R L R L R L R L R L

17.   L R L R L R L R L R L R L R L R

18.   R R L L R R L L R R L L R R L L

19.   L L R R L L R R L L R R L L R R

20.   R L R R L R L L R L R R L R L L

EXERCISES 21–25   The five sticking patterns played as sixteenth notes against BD quarter notes, HH on "2" and "4."

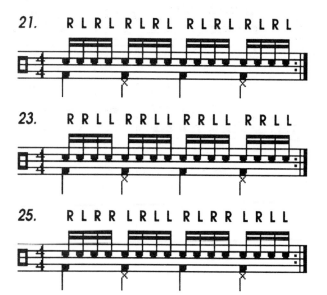

21.   R L R L R L R L R L R L R L R L

22.   L R L R L R L R L R L R L R L R

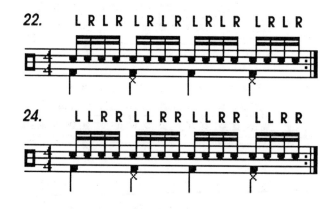

23.   R R L L R R L L R R L L R R L L

24.   L L R R L L R R L L R R L L R R

25.   R L R R L R L L R L R R L R L L

Lesson 12: Sixteenth Rests

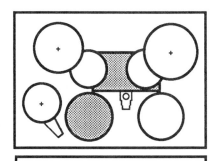

Sixteenth Rests

The sixteenth rest looks like this: $\boxed{\text{ⅲ}}$ It has the same time value as a sixteenth note. Like all rests, you should give it the same attention you would give a note. Count it, but do not play it. If the following exercises seem difficult, play them slowly at first.

45

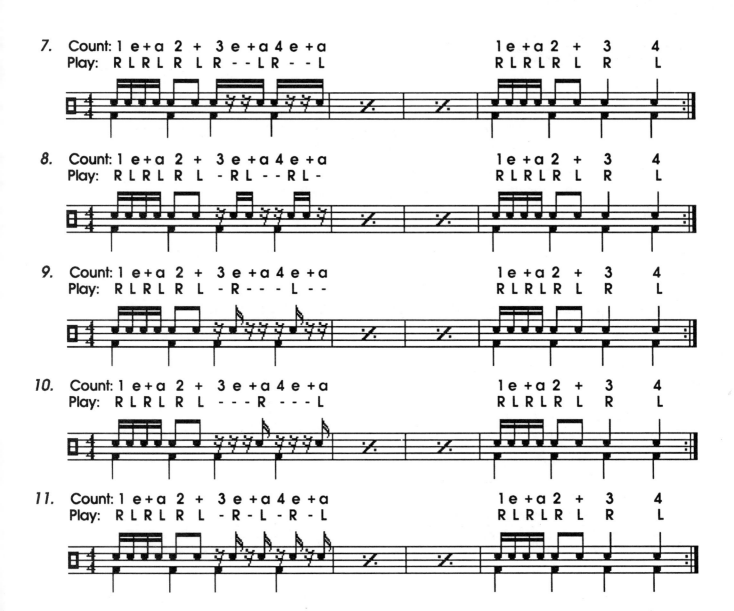

Lesson 13: Sixteenth- and Eighth- Note Combinations

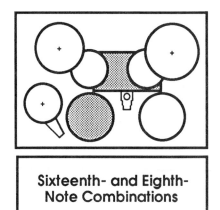

In this lesson, we will look at some sixteenth- and eighth-note combinations.

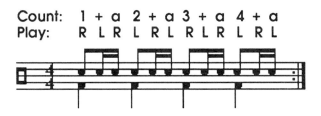 This figure is a combination of **one eighth note and two sixteenth notes.** The first eighth note of the count is unchanged. The second eighth-note count (the "+") is broken down into two sixteenth notes. This figure is played and counted as follows:

Count: 1 + a 2 + a 3 + a 4 + a
Play: R L R L R L R L R L R L

Try the following exercises:

1. Count: 1 + 2 + 3 + a 4 + a   1 + 2 + 3   4
   Play: R L R L R L R L R L   R L R L R   L

2. Count: 1 e + a 2 + a 3 + a 4   +   1 e + a 2 + a 3 + 4
   Play: R L R L R L R L R L R   L   R L R L R L R L R L

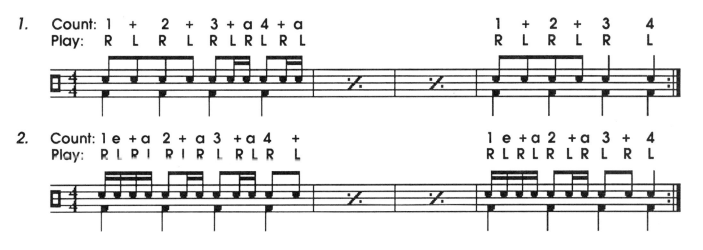

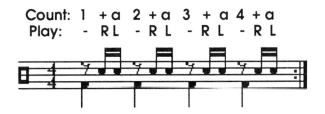 This figure is a combination of **one eighth rest and two sixteenth notes.** The first eighth-note count is **rested.** The second eighth note (the "+") is broken down into two sixteenth notes. This figure is played and counted as follows:

Count: 1 + a 2 + a 3 + a 4 + a
Play: - R L - R L - R L - R L

Now try the following exercises:

3.

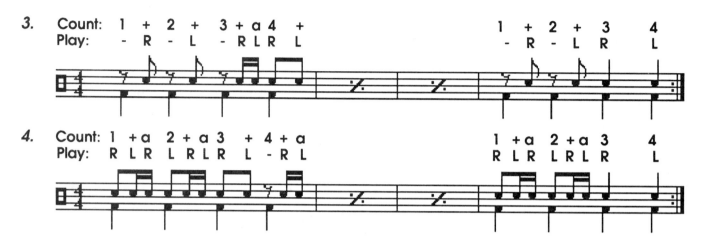

4.

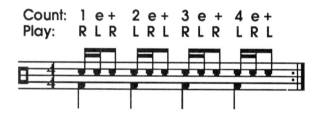
This figure is a combination of **two sixteenth notes and one eighth note.** The first eighth note of the count is broken down into two sixteenth notes, while the second eighth-note count (the "+") is unchanged. This figure is played and counted as follows:

Now try these exercises:

5.

6.

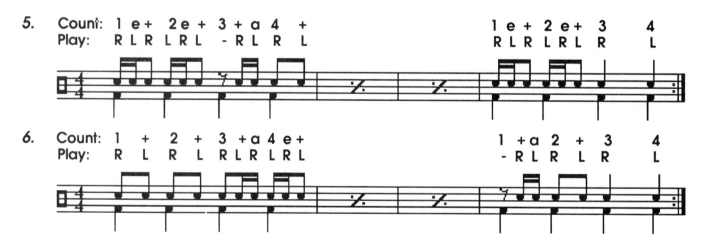

This figure is a combination of **two sixteenth notes and one eighth rest.** The first eighth-note count is broken down into two sixteenth notes, while the second eighth-note count (the "+") is **rested.** This figure is played and counted as follows:

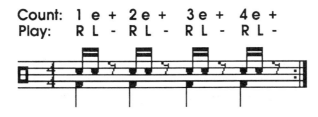

```
Count:  1 e + 2 e +  3 e +  4 e +
Play:   R L - R L -  R L -  R L -
```

Try these exercises:

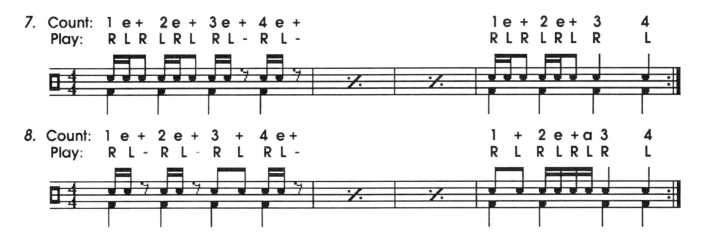

```
7. Count:  1 e + 2 e + 3 e + 4 e +          1 e + 2 e + 3      4
   Play:   R L R L R L R L - R L -          R L R L R L R      L
```

```
8. Count:  1 e + 2 e + 3 + 4 e +            1 + 2 e + a 3      4
   Play:   R L - R L - R L R L -            R L R L R L R      L
```

Look at this figure closely. This is also a combination of **two sixteenths and one eighth note,** but with the first sixteenth count **rested.** This figure is played and counted as follows:

```
Count:  1 e + 2 e + 3 e + 4 e +
Play:   - R L - R L - R L - R L
```

Now try these two exercises:

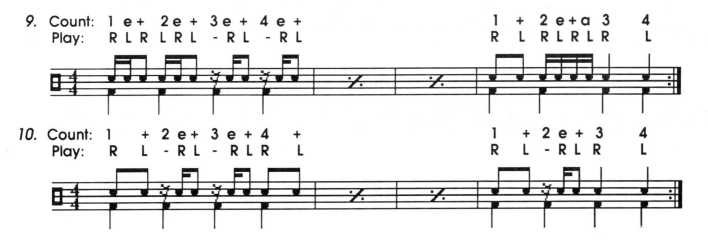

```
9.  Count:  1 e + 2 e + 3 e + 4 e +         1 + 2 e + a 3     4
    Play:   R L R L R L - R L - R L         R L R L R L R     L
```

```
10. Count:  1   + 2 e + 3 e + 4   +         1 + 2 e + 3       4
    Play:   R   L - R L - R L R   L         R L - R L R       L
```

49

COMBINATION EXERCISE The following 32-measure study features combinations of sixteenth notes and eighth notes. The sticking and counting are up to you. Make sure you can play this exercise accurately before you proceed. Refer to the cassette.

Review Worksheet

Look at the chart below and answer the following questions:

Whole Note	
Half Notes	
Quarter Notes	
Eighth Notes	
Sixteenth Notes	

1. One whole note is equal to _____ quarter notes.

2. Eighth notes are twice as fast as _____ notes.

3. Sixteenth notes are twice as fast as _____ notes.

4. One half note is equal to _____ eighth notes.

5. _____ notes are twice as slow as eighth notes.

6. One whole note is equal to _____ sixteenth notes.

7. Each figure below is equivalent to one beat in 4/4 time. Write your own four-measure solo below, using the figures below, in any combination. Be sure you are able to play what you write.

Lesson 14: Two-Handed Sixteenth-Note Rock Beats

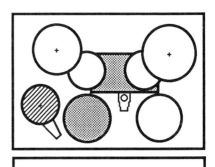

Two-Handed Sixteenth-Note Rock Beats

In this lesson, we will look at rock beats with a sixteenth-note ride pattern. Although sixteenth-note rock beats can be played with one hand on the hi-hat, they can also be played in a two-handed fashion: RLRL, RLRL, RLRL, RLRL, etc.

1. This beat has all the sixteenth notes played on the hi-hat.

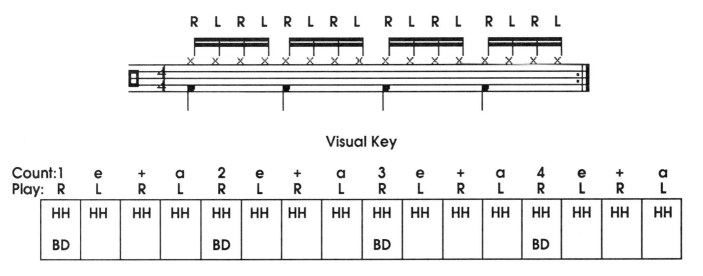

Visual Key

Count:1	e	+	a	2	e	+	a	3	e	+	a	4	e	+	a
Play: R	L	R	L	R	L	R	L	R	L	R	L	R	L	R	L
HH	HH	HH	HH	HH	HH	HH	HH	HH	HH	HH	HH	HH	HH	HH	HH
BD				BD				BD				BD			

2. This pattern has the backbeat on the snare, played with the **right stick**.

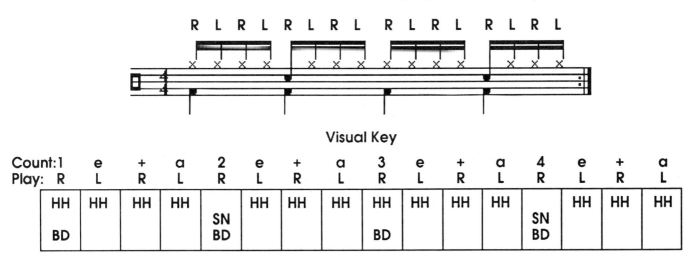

Visual Key

Count:1	e	+	a	2	e	+	a	3	e	+	a	4	e	+	a
Play: R	L	R	L	R	L	R	L	R	L	R	L	R	L	R	L
HH	HH	HH	HH		HH	HH	HH	HH	HH	HH	HH		HH	HH	HH
BD				SN BD				BD				SN BD			

Beats 1 and 2 are predominantly used in the next chart you will learn, so it is to your benefit to learn them well now.

3. This pattern is rhythmically the same as beat 2, the difference being the open hi-hats. When you realize that your feet are moving simultaneously here, it's not so hard to do.

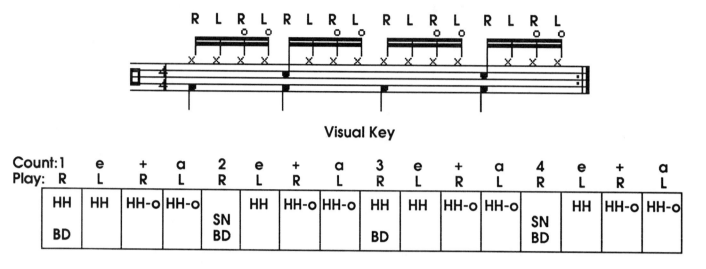

Visual Key

Count:	1	e	+	a	2	e	+	a	3	e	+	a	4	e	+	a
Play:	R	L	R	L	R	L	R	L	R	L	R	L	R	L	R	L
	HH	HH	HH-o	HH-o	SN	HH	HH-o	HH-o	HH	HH	HH-o	HH-o	SN	HH	HH-o	HH-o
	BD				BD				BD				BD			

4. In this situation, both hands are coming off the hi-hat at certain points to play the snare. Make sure there is plenty of room for your hands to maneuver around each other.

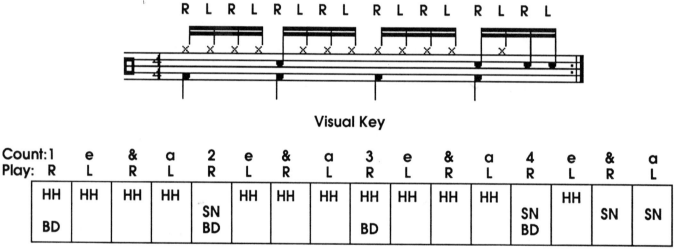

Visual Key

Count:	1	e	&	a	2	e	&	a	3	e	&	a	4	e	&	a
Play:	R	L	R	L	R	L	R	L	R	L	R	L	R	L	R	L
	HH	HH	HH	HH	SN	HH	HH	HH	HH	HH	HH	HH	SN	HH	SN	SN
	BD				BD				BD				BD			

5. This last sixteenth-note rock beat also utilizes both hands on the snare. It might be helpful to realize that, in all the above beats, there should be a steady, unbroken flow of sixteenth notes. Make sure your playing and counting are in sync.

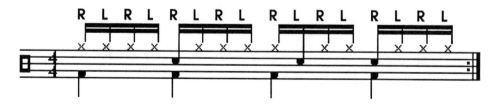

Visual Key

Count:	1	e	&	a	2	e	&	a	3	e	&	a	4	e	&	a
Play:	R	L	R	L	R	L	R	L	R	L	R	L	R	L	R	L
	HH	HH	HH	HH	SN	HH	HH	HH	HH	SN	HH	HH	SN	HH	HH	HH
	BD				BD				BD				BD			

Lesson 15:
Sixteenth-Note Rock
(Chart 3)

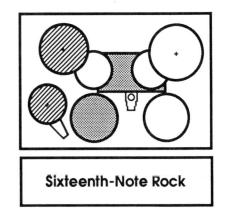

Sixteenth-Note Rock

Preparation

You are now ready for your third chart. Chart 3 is a rock song with a basic feel that is straight sixteenth notes. The basic beat used throughout the chart is one you learned in the last lesson:

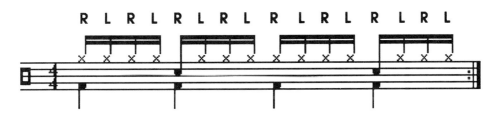

This pattern is used in many styles of rock. Groups such as U2 and INXS have used this beat. On the first line, the pattern is played without the snare backbeat:

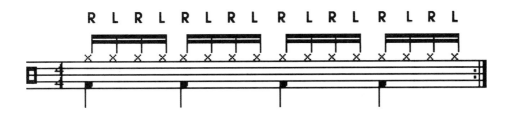

Cymbal crashes are used throughout the chart, and the bass drum plays quarter notes throughout. Here is another look at our legend of notation:

Open Hi-Hat
Hi-Hat (RH)
Bass Drum (RF)
Cymbal Crash
Snare Drum (LH)

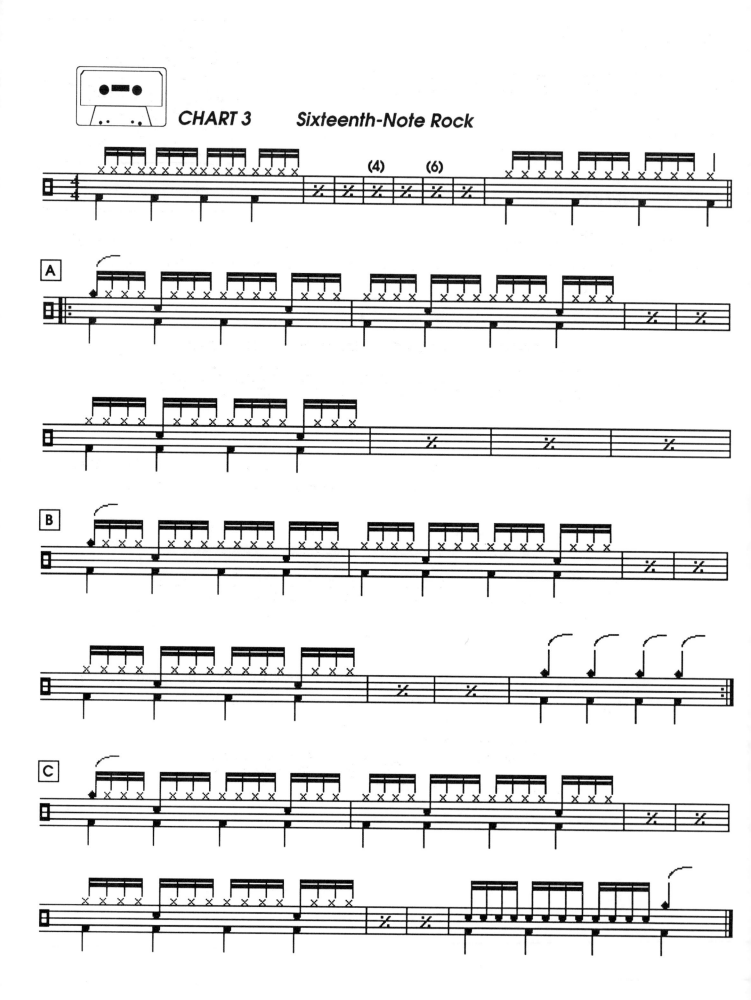

CHART 3   Sixteenth-Note Rock

Lesson 16: Drum Fills

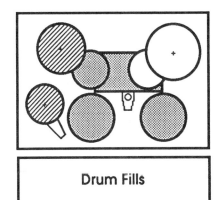

Drum Fills

What is a drum fill? A fill is a rhythmic figure the drummer plays as a change from the time-keeping pattern he or she had been maintaining. Although it is a small break in the pattern, the **tempo is not changed** at all, and in most instances the time-keeping pattern is resumed immediately after the fill. Fills can vary as to style, length, and dynamics. A fill can be soft and subtle, or loud and forceful. An important point to remember is that the flow of the music should not be sacrificed to the technicality of the fill. Actually, most fills are simple in structure and short in duration.

The fills in this lesson are based on this eighth-note rock beat:

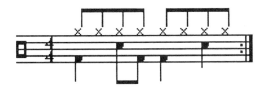

Note on the next page that each eighth-note rock beat is played three complete times, and that the fill occupies part (or all) of the fourth measure. These exercises are written this way for a reason. Most rock music (and most commercial music) is written in verses that are multiples of 4 in length. Therefore, it is important for a drummer to have a sense of what 4 measures "feels" like. If you can feel 4 measures, you can also feel 8, 12, 16, etc.

Fills are used for different reasons, the simplest being that they provide a break in the pattern being played. This break usually comes at the end of a 4-, 8-, 12-, 16-, or 32-measure section. Fills can also be transitional in nature. At the point where one section of a song runs into another (verse to chorus, verse to bridge, chorus to instrumental solo, etc.), a fill can be a useful pivotal point. Because fills can be a point of transition, they can also be considered musical "cues" to the listener that something new is coming up.

Legend of Notation: Two additions are made in our legend of notation. The high tom (usually mounted on the bass drum in front of the snare drum) and low tom (usually called a "floor tom" if it has legs; usually sits to the right of the snare drum):

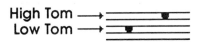

High Tom
Low Tom

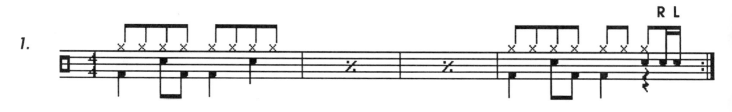

1.

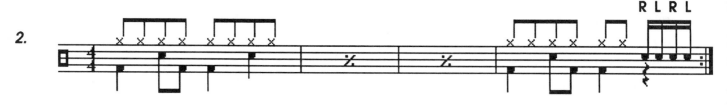

2.

3.

4.

5.

6.

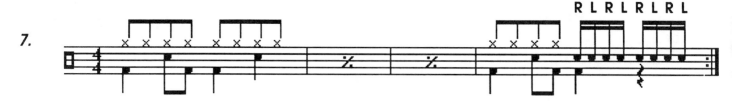

7.

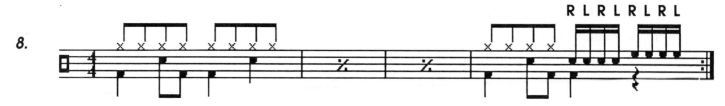

8.

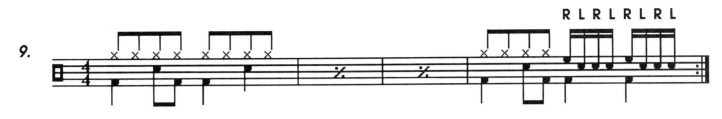

9.

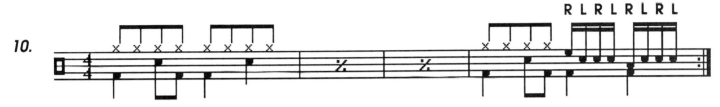

10.

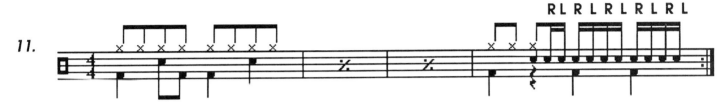

11.

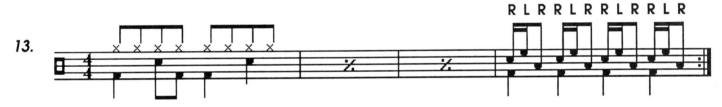

12.

13.

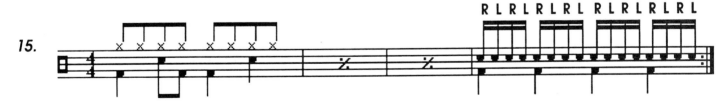

14.

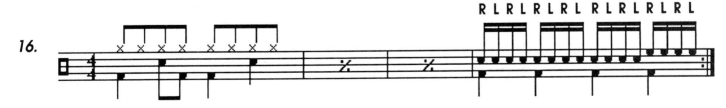

15.

16.

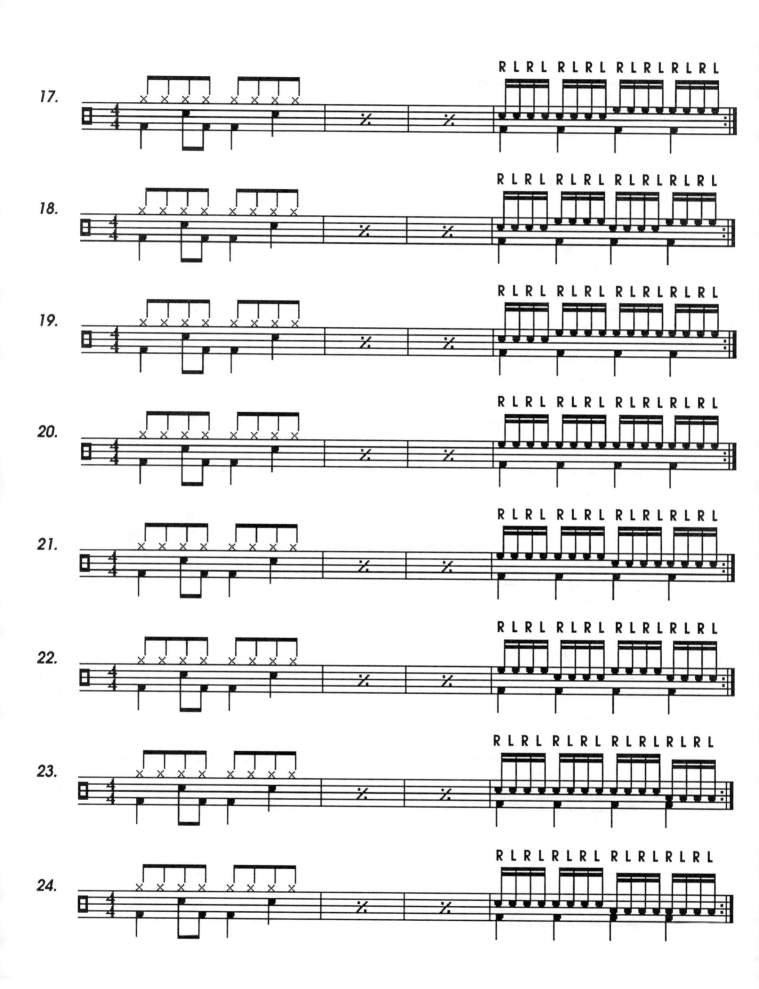

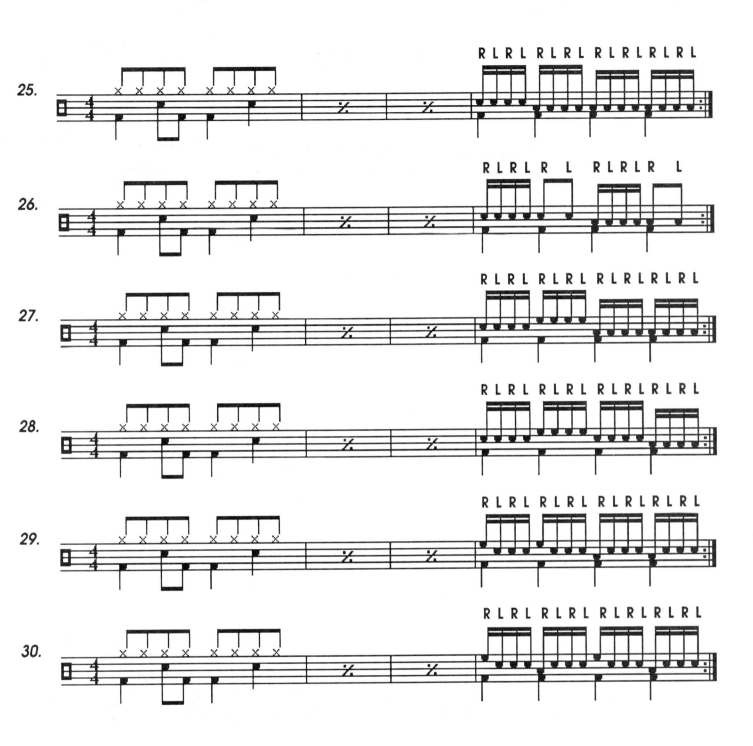

For further study on playing fills, I suggest my book *Killer Fillers,* published by Mel Bay Publications, Inc.

Lesson 17: Dotted Notes and Ties

In this lesson, we will look at two notational devices that alter the value of notes. One such device is the **dotted note.** Sometimes, in reading music, you will see a note with a dot after it. The dot represents **half** the value of the preceding note. The value of the note and the value of the dot are **combined** for a new value. The dotted note is now worth 1½ times the original note's value. Here are some analogies that might help your understanding:

• If an inch were a note, and it was dotted, it would now be 1½ inches.

• If a 10-year-old boy were a note, and he was dotted, he would now be 15 years old.

Now let's look at some commonly used dotted notes.

Dotted half note: Half the value of a half note is a quarter note. Therefore, in 4/4 time, a dotted half note is three beats long:

1. Count: 1 2 3 4   1 2 3 4   1 2 3 4   1 + 2 e + a 3 4
   Play: R - - L   R - - L   R - - L   R L R L R L R L

Dotted quarter note: Half the value of a quarter note is an eighth note. Therefore, a dotted quarter note is equal to three eighth notes in value:

62

2. Count: 1   2 + 3   4   1   2 + 3   4   1   2 + 3   4   1   2   3   4
    Play: R   - L   R   L   R   - L   R   L   R   - L   R   L   R   L   R   L

3. Count: 1   2   3 + 4   1   2   3 + 4   1   2   3 + 4   1   2   3   4
    Play: R   L   R L - R   L   R L - R   L   R L - R   L   R   L

4. Count: 1   2 + 3   4   1   2 + 3   4   1   2 + 3   4   1   2 + 3   4
    Play: R   - L - R   L - R - L   R - L - R   L - R - L

Dotted eighth note: Half the value of an eighth note is a sixteenth note. Therefore, a dotted eighth note is equal to ¾ of a quarter note (or three sixteenth notes):

Dotted eighth and sixteenth note: Look at this figure closely. This combination of a dotted eighth and a sixteenth note is **very** common in reading rhythms. This figure is played and counted as follows:

Count: 1 e+a 2 e+a 3 e+a 4 e+a
Play: R - - L R - - L R - - L R - - L

5. Count: 1e+a   2e+a   3e+a 4   +   1 e+a 2   + 3e+a 4   +
    Play: R L R L R L R L R - - L R   L   R L R L R   L   R - - L R   L

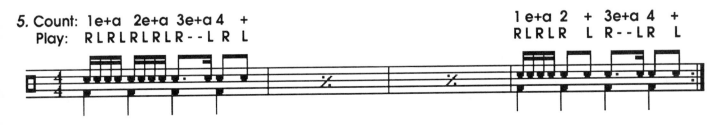

6. Count: 1e+a 2 + 3e+ 4 +   1e+a 2 + 3   4
    Play: R - - L R   L - R L R L   R - - L R   L R   L

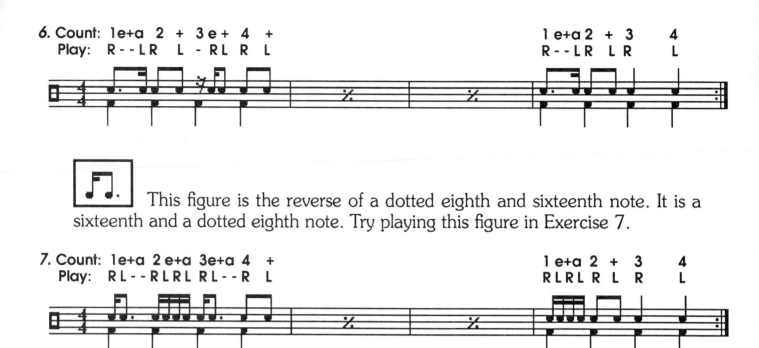

This figure is the reverse of a dotted eighth and sixteenth note. It is a sixteenth and a dotted eighth note. Try playing this figure in Exercise 7.

7. Count: 1e+a 2 e+a 3e+a 4 +   1 e+a 2 + 3   4
    Play: R L - - R L R L R L - - R   L   R L R L R   L   R   L

The tie: A tie is a curved line joining two notes on the same line or space of the staff. A tie has the effect of joining two notes. The value of both notes are joined for their combined value. I like to think of the two tied notes as now one note of a certain length.

8. Count: 1   2   3   4   1   2   3   4   1   2   3   4   1   +   2 e +a 3   4
    Play: R   -   -   L   R   -   -   L   R   -   -   L   R   L   R L R L R   L

(Compare Exercise 8 with Exercise 1. It is possible to write the same rhythm in different ways.)

9. Count: 1   2   3 + 4   1   2   3 + 4   1   2   3 + 4   1   2   3   4
    Play: R   L   R L -   R   L   R L -   R   L   R L -   R   L   R   L

(Compare Exercise 9 with Exercise 3.)

A tie can cross a bar line, as in this exercise:

10. Count: 1   2   3   4   1   2   3   4 + 1   2   3 e +a 4 +   1   2   3   4
     Play: R   -   L   -   -   R   L   R L R   L   R L R L R L   -   R   L   -

Lesson 18: Sixteenth-Eighth-Sixteenth Combination

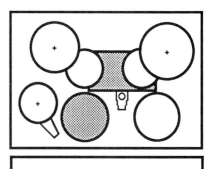

Sixteenth-Eighth-Sixteenth Combination

In Lesson 13, you learned to read and play eighth- and sixteenth-note combination figures. In this lesson, we will look at another combination figure:

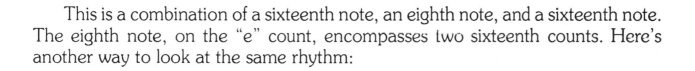

This is a combination of a sixteenth note, an eighth note, and a sixteenth note. The eighth note, on the "e" count, encompasses two sixteenth counts. Here's another way to look at the same rhythm:

Of the four sixteenth-note counts, the "+" is not played. This figure is usually played and counted like this:

```
Count:  1 e + a 2 e - a 3 e - a 4 e -a
Play:   R L   L R L   L R L   L R L   L
```

Now try these exercises:

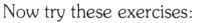

1. Count: 1 + 2 + 3 + 4 e + a   1 + 2 + 3 4
   Play: R L R L R L R L L   R L R L R L

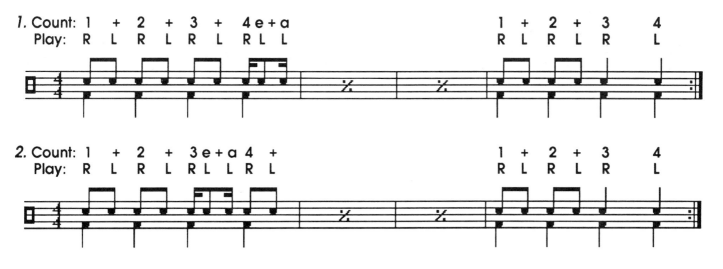

2. Count: 1 + 2 + 3 e + a 4 +   1 + 2 + 3 4
   Play: R L R L R L L L R L   R L R L R L

Lesson 19: Advanced Eighth-Note Rock Beats

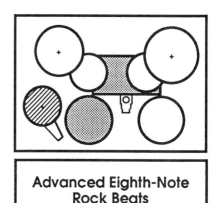

Advanced Eighth-Note Rock Beats

In this lesson, we will look at eighth-note rock beats that are more complex. Now that we have learned sixteenth- and eighth-note combinations, as well as dotted notes, we will now incorporate those figures on the bass drum and snare, against a steady eighth-note hi-hat ride pattern. Some of these notes will fall between the hi-hat eighth notes, as well as coinciding with them. Make sure that the bass-drum and snare figures are placed accurately, and make sure the hi-hat keeps a steady rhythm.

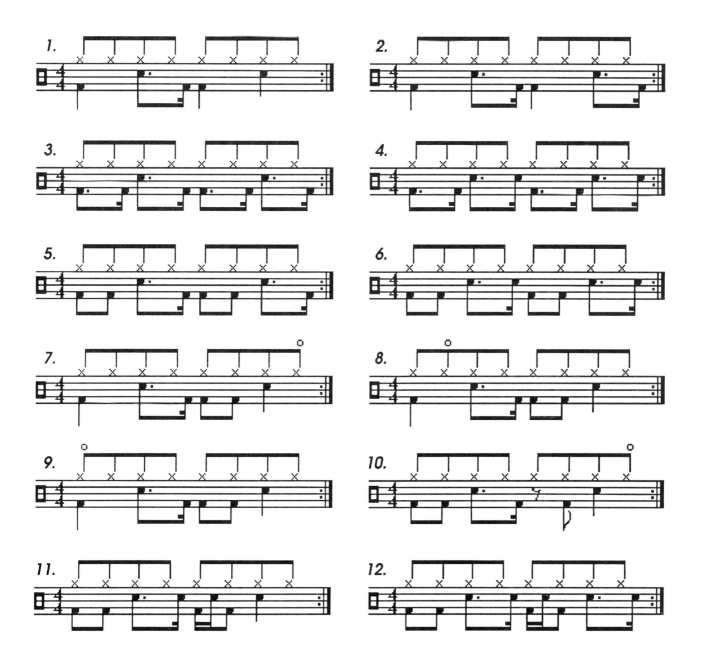

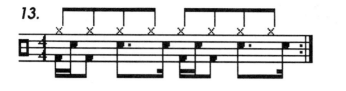

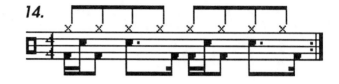

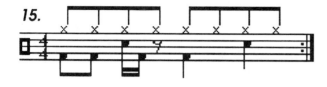

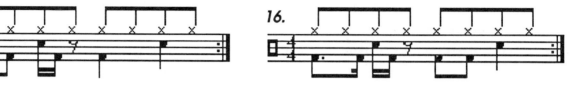

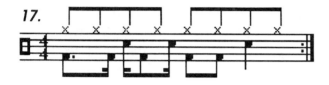

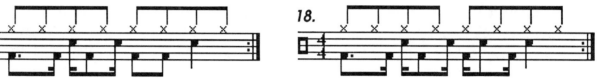

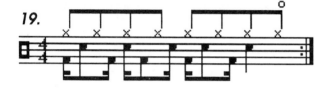

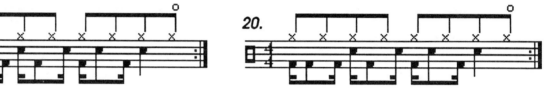

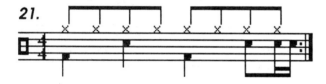

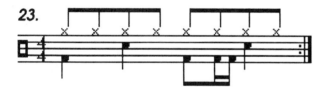

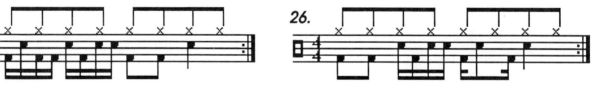

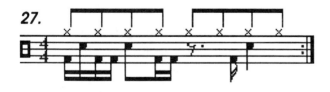

31.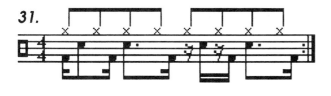

32.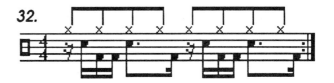

33.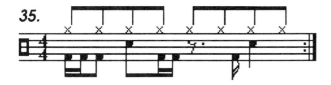

34.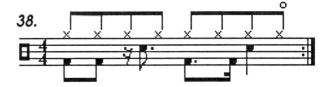

35.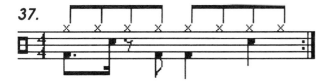

36.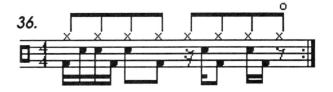

37.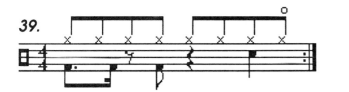

38.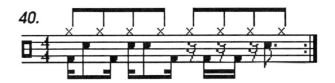

39.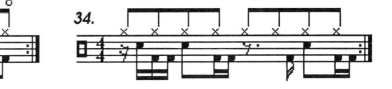

40.

Lesson 20: Accents and Syncopation

Accents

This is an accent: > . When placed over or under a note, that note is to be played with more emphasis and volume than its surrounding notes. The accented note should "stick out" from among the others.

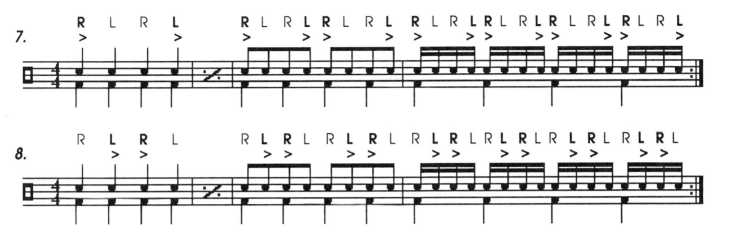

What Is Syncopation?

Syncopation is a term used describe a rhythm in which an accent is placed on a note where none is usually expected. Every kind of time signature (2/4, 3/4, 4/4, etc.) has a natural principal accent on the first beat. In longer measures like 4/4, there is a secondary accent on the second half of the measure. If an accent is placed on a beat or count other than the natural accents (like Exercise 2 on the previous page), syncopation will occur. Syncopation adds rhythmic excitement to music.

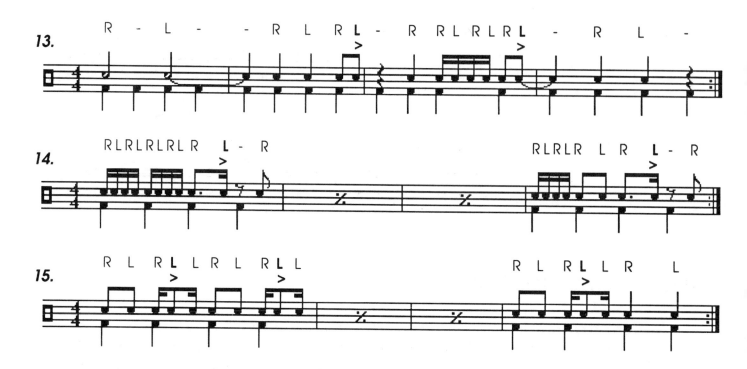

Assignment: Place accents wherever you want them in the following eight-measure exercise. Then play it!

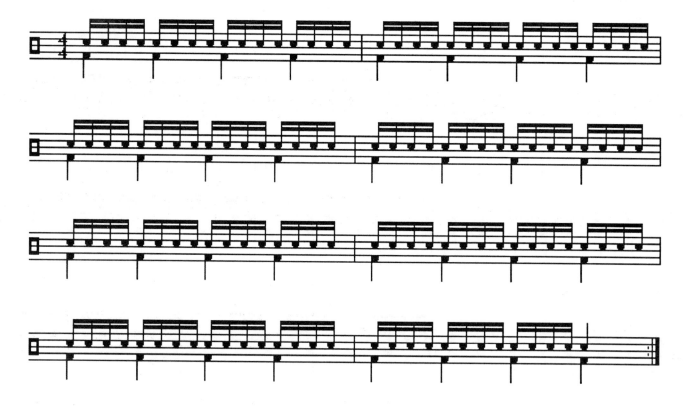

Set Application: Take all the exercises in this lesson and, along with the snare and bass-drum parts, place the accents on the toms. Place LH accents on the high tom, RH accents on the floor tom.

Lesson 21: Medium Funk (Chart 4)

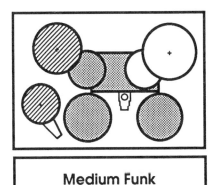

Medium Funk

Preparation

Here we have our most challenging chart so far. Chart 4 is in a medium funk style. The beats used here are like those you learned in Lesson 19, and the rhythms involve **syncopation,** which you just learned about in Lesson 20. Here is the legend of notation, which you should have about memorized by now:

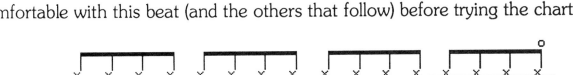

There is a two-measure pattern that is used in the **introduction** (the first four measures) and throughout *A*. Note the quarter rest on the first beat of the second measure. This is another example of syncopation. Spend a few minutes getting comfortable with this beat (and the others that follow) before trying the chart.

At *B*, the beat gets a little busier:

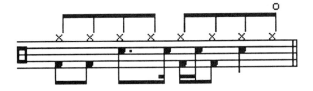

73

At the end of *B*, there are first and second endings (the first ending repeats back to the beginning of *A)* with a drum fill in each of them. Here are the suggested stickings:

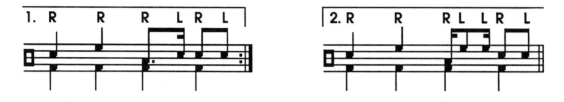

At *C*, there is another two-measure pattern, quite syncopated. The chart finishes on this pattern.

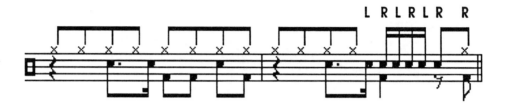

CHART 4   Medium Funk

Lesson 22: Quarter-Note Rock Beats

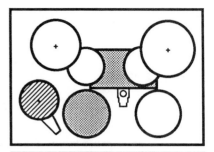

Quarter-Note Rock Beats

So far we have seen rock beats based on both eighth-note and sixteenth-note ride patterns. Another frequently used ride pattern utilizes quarter notes. This pattern is useful if the tempo is fast or if the overall feel of the music calls for driving quarter notes.

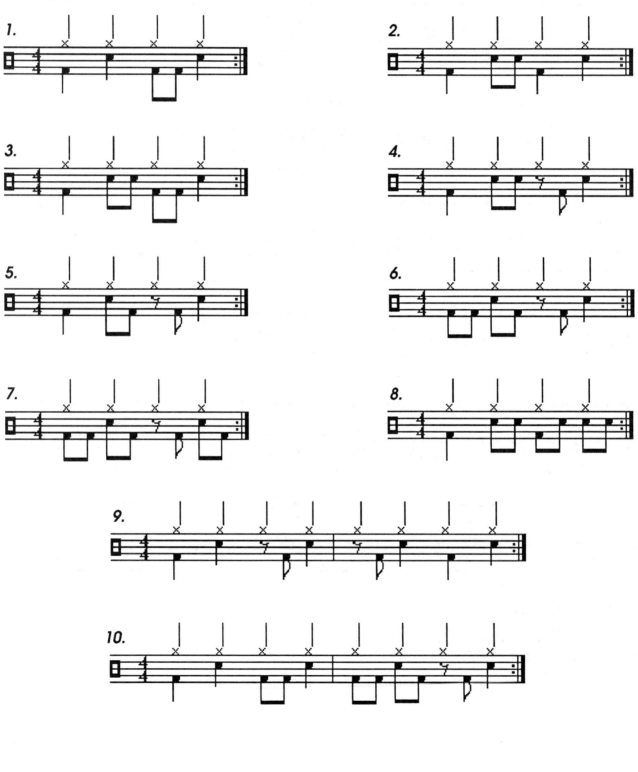

Lesson 23:
Eighth-Note Triplets

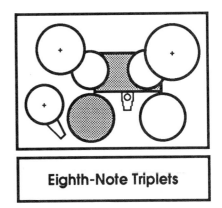

Eighth-Note Triplets

Triplet: A triplet consists of three notes of equal value played in the same time value as two like notes normally have. A triplet is indicated by the number "3" placed over the three notes.

Eighth-Note Triplet: Normally, one quarter note equals two eighth notes. An eighth-note triplet consists of three equal eighth notes played evenly in the same time value as two regular eighth notes. Therefore, one quarter note equals an eighth-note triplet:

Look at it this way:

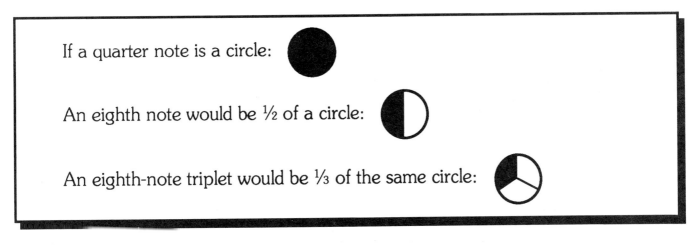

If a quarter note is a circle:

An eighth note would be ½ of a circle:

An eighth-note triplet would be ⅓ of the same circle:

Eighth-note triplets can be played and counted as follows:

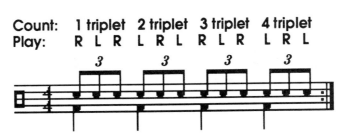

Now try these exercises:

A triplet note, like any other note, can be rested. Watch the sticking.

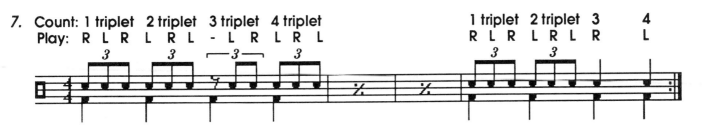

7. Count: 1 triplet 2 triplet 3 triplet 4 triplet   1 triplet 2 triplet 3   4
   Play: R L R   L R L   - L R   L R L   R L R   L R L R   L

Here, eighth-note triplets are played alongside regular eighth notes. Watch the shift in the feeling and in the counting, and keep your bass drum steady.

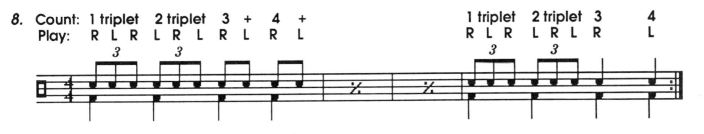

8. Count: 1 triplet 2 triplet 3 + 4 +   1 triplet 2 triplet 3   4
   Play: R L R   L R L   R L R L   R L R   L R L R   L

Lesson 24: Triplet Beats

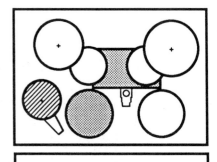

Triplet Beats

The following beats are based on eighth-note triplets and are appropriate for slow blues songs and rock ballads.

1.

Count: 1 triplet   2 triplet   3 triplet   4 triplet

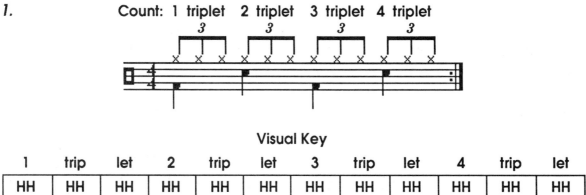

Visual Key

1	trip	let	2	trip	let	3	trip	let	4	trip	let
HH	HH	HH	HH SN	HH	HH	HH	HH	HH	HH SN	HH	HH
BD						BD					

2.

Count: 1 triplet   2 triplet   3 triplet   4 triplet

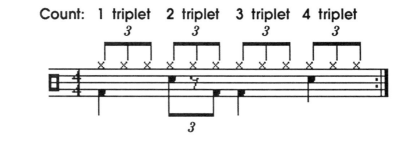

Visual Key

1	trip	let	2	trip	let	3	trip	let	4	trip	let
HH	HH	HH	HH SN	HH	HH	HH	HH	HH	HH SN	HH	HH
BD					BD	BD					

3.

Count: 1 triplet   2 triplet   3 triplet   4 triplet

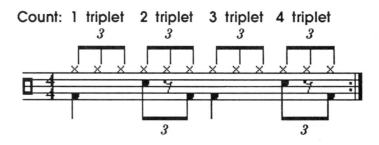

80

1	trip	let	2	trip	let	3	trip	let	4	trip	let
HH	HH	HH	HH SN	HH	HH	HH	HH	HH	HH SN	HH	HH
BD					BD	BD					BD

4.   Count: 1 triplet   2 triplet   3 triplet   4 triplet

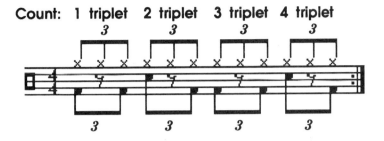

Visual Key

1	trip	let	2	trip	let	3	trip	let	4	trip	let
HH	HH	HH	HH SN	HH	HH	HH	HH	HH	HH SN	HH	HH
BD		BD			BD	BD		BD			BD

5.   Count: 1 triplet   2 triplet   3 triplet   4 triplet

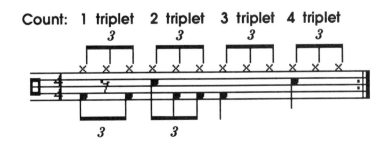

Visual Key

1	trip	let	2	trip	let	3	trip	let	4	trip	let
HH	HH	HH	HH SN	HH	HH	HH	HH	HH	HH SN	HH SN	HH
BD		BD			BD	BD		BD			BD

6.   Count: 1 triplet   2 triplet   3 triplet   4 triplet

Visual Key

1	trip	let	2	trip	let	3	trip	let	4	trip	let
HH	HH	HH	HH SN	HH	HH	HH	HH	HH	HH SN	HH	HH
BD		BD		BD	BD	BD					

Lesson 25:
Slow Blues (Chart 5)

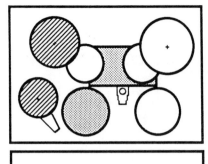

Slow Blues

Preparation

Chart 5 is a typical slow blues in the 12-bar blues form. (Remember Chart 1?) There is basically one slow triplet drum pattern used throughout:

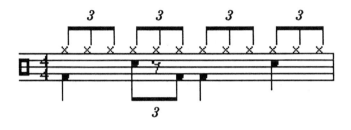

At the end of the first line (the introduction) and at the end of the last line (the ending) there is this measure:

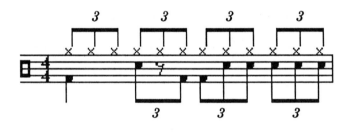

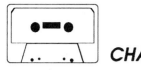

CHART 5 *Slow Blues*

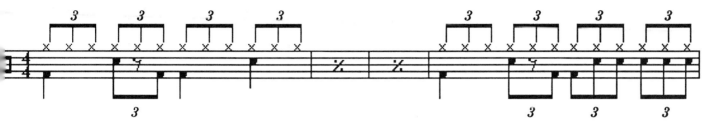

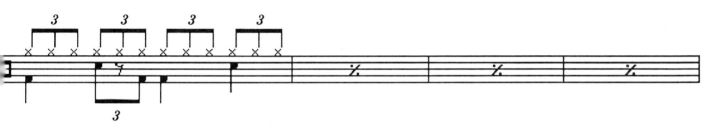

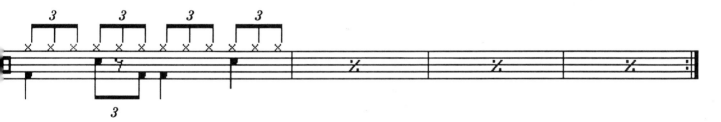

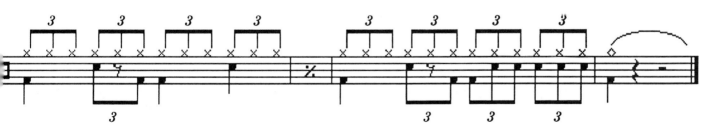

Lesson 26:
Shuffle Beats

In this lesson, you will learn to play the **shuffle,** a pattern based on **triplets.** To get the feel of a shuffle, first play this triplet pattern. Play the sticking as indicated.

Count:	1 triplet	2 triplet	3 triplet	4 triplet
Play:	R L R	R L R	R L R	R L R

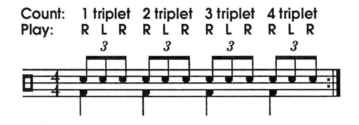

Now play the same pattern, with the left hand taken out:

Count:	1 triplet	2 triplet	3 triplet	4 triplet
Play:	R - R	R - R	R - R	R - R

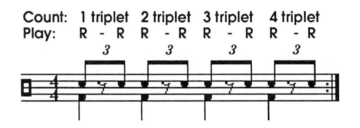

Now transfer this right-hand pattern to the hi-hat:

Count:	1 triplet	2 triplet	3 triplet	4 triplet
Play:	R - R	R - R	R - R	R - R

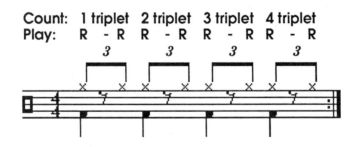

The shuffle is a "skipping" rhythm that should flow smoothly. Change the counting to this, which is less cumbersome:

Count:	1	ah	2	ah	3	ah	4		ah
Play:	R	-	R	R	-	R	R	-	R	R	-	R

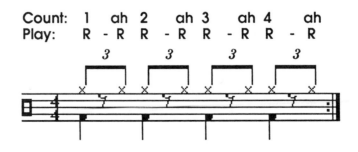

84

1.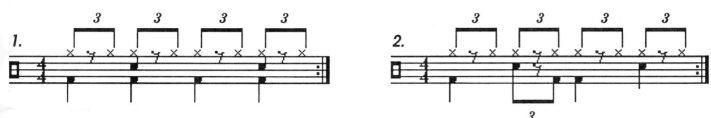

2.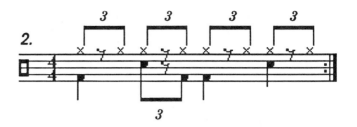

3.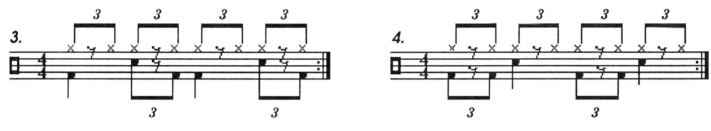

4.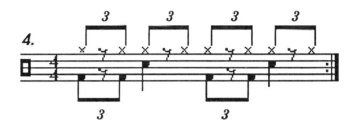

5.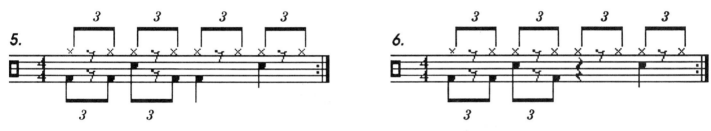

6.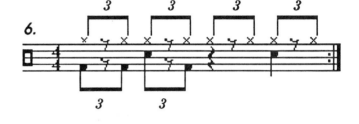

7.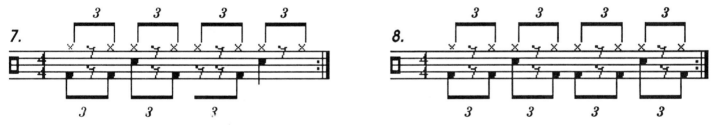

8.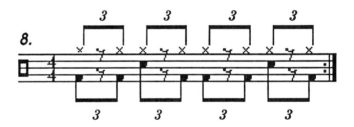

Lesson 27:
Medium Shuffle (Chart 6)

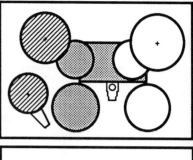

Medium Shuffle

Preparation

Well, here we are at the last lesson, with a final chart.
Chart 6 is a medium-tempo shuffle, and a standard shuffle beat with the bass drum playing quarter notes (pattern #1 on the previous page) is used throughout the chart:

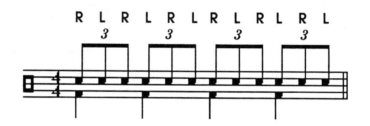

At the end of the first line, there is a full measure of triplets:

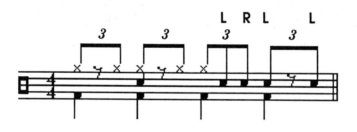

At the eighth measure of sections *A* and *B,* there is this fill:

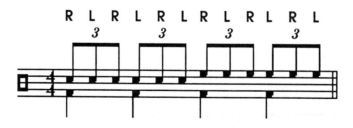

At the end of the chart, there is this triplet fill on the snare and high tom:

CHART 6 Medium Shuffle

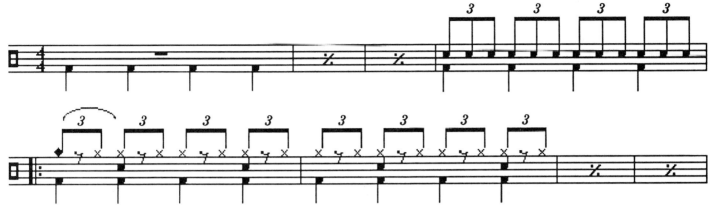

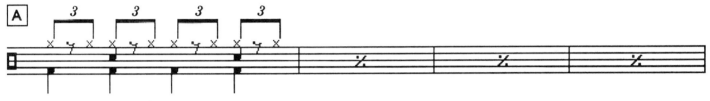

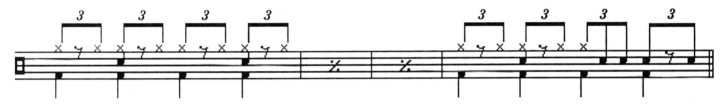

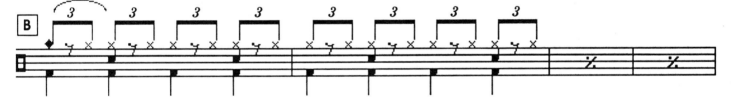

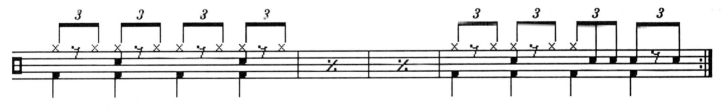

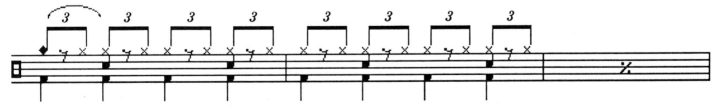

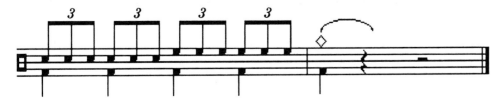

Suggestions for Successful Drumming

• **_Learn another instrument._** I suggest piano, as the scales, melodies, and chords are **tangible** and **graphic**. In other words, everything is laid out for you to see, touch, and hear at the same time, thereby allowing you to understand musical ideas with your eyes, hands, and ears. Most successful musicians have a working knowledge of the keyboard, and the benefits to you as a drummer are both direct and indirect:

a. As your ear becomes more perceptive, you become more aware of what other musicians are doing, so you can react in a musical way.

b. You can follow charts more easily (lead sheets as well as drum charts).

c. You understand **form** in music more easily.

d. You can communicate with musicians in a succinct way.

e. You can even write your own songs. Many great drummers are also known as composers: Louie Bellson, Jack DeJohnette, Billy Cobham, etc.

• **_Learn other styles of music._** If you are a rock drummer, study jazz and Latin patterns. Likewise, if you are a jazz drummer, it will be helpful if you study current rock styles. Not only will your versatility make you more in demand with a greater number of musicians, but the coordinational skills you develop in one style will carry over into another. Many of the top rock drummers around today also have a strong jazz background, and it shows in their playing.

• **_Learn to read music._** Music notation is the quickest way to convey a musical idea, whether in the studio, in a performance, or in a rehearsal. This is not to discount playing by ear, which is also important. But there will be instances in which your ear alone will not be sufficient, and your understanding of music notation will clear up any confusion. Actually, a good musician uses the eyes and the ears in conjunction with each other. Being able to read, by itself, will not necessarily make you a better musician, but it is like having one more important tool in your tool box. You will be better prepared to "fix things."

There are also indirect benefits to being a proficient reader, and one of them is that you begin to hear and think in terms of notation. This soon translates into your being aware of the placement, accuracy, and phrasing of everything you play, whether or not you are actually reading music at the time. As your reading skills improve, you also become available for gigs that require reading.

• **Gain experience.** This usually means, at first, to play anytime, anywhere, with anybody! No matter how much you study and practice, your development as a musician is incomplete without some "on-the-job experience." There are simply some things that can't be learned except by performing with other musicians. So do what you can toward this end, whether playing in rock bands, school bands, community concert bands, etc. With experience will come increased confidence. The more contacts you have through playing with others, the greater your chances are of "moving up" to better gigs. Good luck!

Everybody's Music Teacher